D0811755

Physics and Biology

Physics and Biology

M. V. VOLKENSTEIN

Institute of Molecular Biology
Academy of Sciences of the USSR
Moscow, USSR

1982

ACADEMIC PRESS

A Subsidiary of Harcourt Brace Jovanovich, Publishers

New York London
Paris San Diego San Francisco São Paulo Sydney Tokyo Toronto

ACADEMIC PRESS, INC.
111 Fifth Avenue, New York, New York 10003

United Kingdom Edition published by
ACADEMIC PRESS, INC. (LONDON) LTD.
24/28 Oval Road, London NW1 7DX

Library of Congress Cataloging in Publication Data

Vol′kenshteĭn, M. V. (Mikhail Vladimirovich), date.
Physics and biology.

Bibliography: p.
Includes index.
1. Biophysics. I. Title.
QH505.V643 1982 574.19'1 82-8848
ISBN 0-12-723140-4 AACR2

PRINTED IN THE UNITED STATES OF AMERICA

82 83 84 85 9 8 7 6 5 4 3 2 1

PHYSICS AND BIOLOGY. Translated from the original Russian edition entitled FIZIKA I BIOLOGIYA, published by Nauka, Moscow, 1980.

Contents

Preface

This small book is intended for those readers who want to be acquainted with some important problems in the contemporary natural sciences that are related to biophysics. As a result of the great developments in biology, physics, and chemistry, there has begun the building of biological physics, i.e., the science that studies life from the viewpoint of the laws and methods of experimental and theoretical physics. This basis has proved to be reliable: biophysics has already added to the understanding of a series of biological phenomena, and it has led to discoveries that are important for both theory and practice. On the one hand biophysics leads to the development of theoretical biology and on the other it is incorporated into medicine, pharmacology, ecology, and agriculture.

One of the main goals of this book is to show the unlimited possibilities of physics in the knowledge of life. However, these possibilities cannot be realized independently of biology (and chemistry). In our time, at a period of integration of the sciences, one must be not only a physicist, biologist, or chemist, but also a natural scientist in the broad sense of the word. The sciences unite. To study life, it is necessary to know zoology and botany, cytology and physiology.

Genuine biophysics is a rather young science. We often meet with problems whose physical solutions are as yet impossible because of the insufficiency of our biological knowledge. Therefore we should not be surprised by the appearance of speculative and pseudoscientific ideas that pretend to be related to biophysics. Some of these ideas are considered in the last section of the book. Notwithstanding its youth, biophysics can distinguish between truth and its simulation.

In spite of the popular character of the presentation, the reader will repeatedly meet with mathematical formulas in this book. However, a chemist or biologist who is acquainted with elementary courses in physics and mathematics should have no difficulty in understanding the material.

Of course for a deeper acquaintance with biophysics the reader will need other books. Some of them—both the popular and the rather serious ones—are listed at the end of the book.

Critical remarks will be accepted by the author with gratitude.

CHAPTER 1

Contemporary Biophysics

In the beginning of the twentieth century, natural science entered an era of accelerated development. The fundamentals of science—the concepts of space and time, matter and field—underwent tremendous changes. The development of science in the twentieth century has been shaped by the revolution in physics, climaxing with the theory of relativity and with quantum mechanics. The revolution in physics in turn transformed the fundamentals of chemistry: the explanation of Mendeleev's periodic law and the theoretical treatment of chemical bonds and reactions. Physics and chemistry, which previously had combined mainly at the phenomenological level (chemical thermodynamics, theory of solutions, chemical kinetics), became united. Great changes also occurred in the *Weltanschauung* of science: hand in hand with the increasing specialization of knowledge came a strong tendency toward integration.

In the second half of the twentieth century, physics, chemistry, and biology were united in the discipline of molecular biology, which uncovered the physical and chemical essence of the fundamental phenomena of life. Simultaneously, entirely new fields of science, such as cybernetics and information theory, sprang up. The relationship between pure and applied science changed. The gap between theories and their practical applications narrowed. Humanity entered a period of scientific–technical revolution affecting all areas of natural and humanitarian sciences, technics, agriculture, and medicine.

In these conditions, which are unprecedented in human history, the question of the relationship between physics and biology takes on great importance. Are the physical principles and laws, discovered mainly in studies of the objects and phenomena of nonliving nature, sufficient to explain the phenomena of life?

Various answers to this question are possible. The first answer is yes, they are sufficient. The second answer is not so definite: they are not sufficient, but the future development of biophysics, the physics of the life phenomena, will lead to the discovery of completely new physical principles and laws that will not contradict the previous ones. This new physics will form the basis of a scientific explanation of the phenomena of life. The third answer is negative: physics is not and never will be able to explain biological phenomena because they follow purely biological laws, which cannot be explained on a physicochemical basis. This answer comes from the doctrine of vitalism, which was widespread in biology of the last century and which still has some adherents nowadays.

Finally, the ideas of Niels Bohr hold a special place in the solution of the question [1].

Bohr formulated the complementarity principle, according to which the examination of the material world meets with complementary characteristics and notions. For example, in quantum mechanics, the physics of the microworld, the microparticle's coordinate and velocity are complementary, that is, each of these quantities can be measured separately with any precision, but they cannot be measured simultaneously; precise measurement of the electron's position makes the determination of its velocity impossible, and vice versa. The nonexactness of coordinate Δx and velocity Δv is related by Heisenberg's uncertainty principle (see [2])

$$\Delta x \, \Delta v \geq \frac{h}{4\pi m} \tag{1}$$

where m is the mass of electron and $h = 6.62 \times 10^{-27}$ erg sec is Planck's constant. When Δx tends to zero, Δv tends to infinity, and vice versa.

Bohr considered biological laws as complementary to the laws governing nonliving bodies. In other words, it is impossible to study simultaneously the atomic–molecular structure of the cell or organism and its behavior as a total biological system. Bohr considered life the main postulate of biology that cannot be analyzed further, in the same way that the existence of the quantum of action is the nonanalyzable basis of atomic physics [1]. Thus, biology on one hand and physics and chemistry on the other appear to be incompatible, though they do not contradict each other.

Later, Bohr changed his point of view. Instead of the complementarity of the physical sciences with biology, he began to speak of complementarity between physicochemical considerations practically applied to biology and notions which were directly connected with the integrity of organism. Reality is determined not by the postulative character of the notion of life, but by the extreme complexity of the living organism. Not long before his death, Bohr spoke only about practical (and hence surmountable) complementarity of biology and physics [3]. (See also Bohr's letter to the author published in [4].)

Let us return to the starting point. For a serious analysis of the problem it is necessary to determine what physics is.

Physics is the science that studies the structure and properties of concrete types of matter (i.e., substances and fields) and the forms of their existence, of space, and of time. Although this definition is very general, the whole development of physics agrees with it. The main problems of modern physics are in cosmology, the study of the universe—past, present, and future—as a whole, and in elementary particle physics, the study of the microcosmos. These disciplines come together.

Two other fundamental natural sciences are chemistry and biology. Chemistry is the science of the transformations of electronic shells in atoms and molecules during chemical reactions; biology is the science of life phenomena. We see that the definitions of physics, chemistry, and biology are incompatible in the sense that the separation of natural science into these three disciplines is not absolute; the definition of each does not exclude the others. Of course, we have called three great sciences that exist in reality and are intensively developed.

From the general definition of physics, one might think that all other natural sciences, especially chemistry and biology, can be reduced to it. All natural sciences study matter. Do we return to the understanding of physics in its prescientific period, as expressed by Aristotle? Are physics and natural science identical notions?

No, chemistry and biology are characterized by independent methods of research and by laws discovered with their help. In this context the word "reduce" is meaningless. The ideas suggested mean only that physics forms the theoretical basis of all fields of natural science. The establishment of this theoretical basis means the deepening of every science, the investigation of the fundamental laws that explain the phenomena it examines. In chemistry this basis has been already established. In biology, which studies much more complicated phenomena, it has not; but proceeding from the given definition of physics, we must conclude that physics will be the basis of the theoretical biology of the future.

However, this statement is completely insufficient, for it is based only on general reasoning. For the consideration of the relationship of physics and biology, it is necessary to investigate the following: What does physics give to biology now? How does physics answer the questions about the essence of life phenomena? How did biophysics develop? Does biophysics meet with principal difficulties and limitations? As will be shown further, there is reason to suggest that modern physics is sufficient for the understanding of biological phenomena. Stated differently, there is no limit to the application of existing physics to biology. Hence there is no reason to think that biology will require the creation of a new physics.

There have indeed been situations in science that have required the creation of a new physics. The theory of relativity was constructed because classic electrodynamics could not explain the contradictions that appeared in the examination of electromagnetic fields of moving bodies; the famous 1905 paper in which Einstein first formulated the special theory of relativity had the title *Zur Elektrodynamik bewegter Körper*. In a similar way, quantum mechanics was created to overcome the deadlock into which classical physics had fallen while examining the radiation of solid bodies. In both cases, the new theories did not reject the old ones, but included them as a special case.

To solve the problem of the relationship of physics and biology, we must investigate the place occupied by cells and organisms in the enormous hierarchy beginning with elementary particles and ending with the galaxies and the universe as a whole. It is important to identify the main phenomena of life, and their differences from and similarities with the phenomena of nonliving nature. Thanks to the development of biology, today it is not only possible to ask these questions, but to answer them as well, though only partly.

Cells and organisms are macroscopic systems composed of multitudes of atoms and molecules. The smallest cell—the bacterium *Mycoplasma laidlavii*—has a volume 10^9 times greater than that of an atom. Therefore, the biological physics of cells and organisms cannot be directly relationed to the physics of the microworld. The relevance of quantum mechanics to biology is in examining the structure and properties of atoms and molecules that execute biological functions.

Living systems are characterized by two main pecularities. First, they are open systems that exchange matter and energy with the surrounding world. Second, they are historical; each cell and each organism develops and changes in time, and its present state is the result of its individual development and of general evolutionary development.

At this point it is necessary to define life. One of the first scientific definitions, based on the achievements of chemistry and biology of the last century, was suggested by Engels: "Life is the form of existence of the proteinic bodies, the essential feature of which is the constant exchange of substances with the surrounding environment." [5] Two concepts are emphasized in this definition. The first is the determinative role of proteins in life phenomena. This concept has been confirmed by the whole further development of science. As we now know, the proteins are responsible for all processes that take place in a living organism, although other substances are also important for life (especially the nucleic acids, which organize the synthesis of proteins in cells). The second concept contained in the definition of life given by Engels is metabolism, the exchange of substances, which makes the living system an open one.

Let us suggest an expanded definition of a living system based on current knowledge in biology, biochemistry, and biophysics.

The living organism is an open, self-regulated, and self-reproducible system that is far from equilibrium, that develops in an irreversible way and that arises as a result of individual and evolutionary development; it is a heterogeneous system consisting of multifarious big and small molecules. The most important substances in the organism are the biopolymers, big molecules of proteins and nucleic acids.

The heterogeneity of a living organism must be emphasized. There is no such thing as a "living molecule." Despite its complexity, a single molecule of the protein or of the nucleic acid does not live, and in this sense is like the molecule of sugar or CO_2. Obviously, the creation and existence of the systems that correspond to the given definition of life are connected with many problems of physics. If physics must explain the phenomena of life, it must

(i) discover the main laws of behavior of the open nonequilibrium systems, that is, discover a thermodynamic basis of life;

(ii) interpret theoretically the phenomena of evolutionary and individual development;

(iii) explain the phenomena of self-regulation and self-reproduction;

(iv) uncover the nature of biological processes at the atomic–molecular level, that is, discover the connection between the structure and biological function of proteins, nucleic acids, and other substances that act in cells; and research the physical phenomena in living systems at higher overmolecular levels, at the level of cells and organoids forming them;

(v) devise (and provide theoretical explanations for) physical and physicochemical methods of investigation of the biologically functional substances and overmolecular structures built by them; and

(vi) give a physical explanation of a vast complex of physiological phenomena, such as generation and propagation of nerve impulses, muscle contraction, reception of external signals by the sensory organs, and photosynthesis.

Substantial success has been achieved in these six areas. At the same time, science is far from a genuine understanding of the phenomena of life because of the extreme complexity of living systems and the insufficiency of biological, biochemical, and biophysical knowledge. Rigorous formulation of the physical problem, that is, formulation on the basis of general physical laws and atomic–molecular presentation, is now possible in biology only in a limited number of cases. The set of essential biological problems is very far from physics and chemistry. We know almost nothing about the material nature of higher nervous activity, be it memory and thought in higher vertebrates or complicated instinctive behavior in insects.

The items listed above are the subject of biophysics. This science is now changing from an auxiliary part of biology into the very physics of life phenomena. Not all biologists agree with this statement; many of them think that the aim of biophysics is to apply physical methods to biology. This is obviously wrong: From the beginning, biology has used the microscope, a complicated physical device. A much more simple but surely also a physical instrument is the medical thermometer. It makes no sense to say that the application of microscope, thermometer, or even electrocardiograph is biophysics, although one humorous definition of biophysics says that it is the work of a medical doctor who is using a device too complicated for his understanding.

Of course, what branch of science the methods come from is not really important. Biophysical investigations begin with the physical formulation of a problem relating to life phenomena. This problem can be solved by other methods, for example, biological or chemical ones, as long as they are valid scientific procedures.

The interaction of physics and biology is old enough. Descartes sought the explanation of the blood circulation in mechanics, considering the human body as a kind of machine. Similar ideas were developed in Borelli's two-volume treatise *About the motion of animals* (1680–1681). The concepts of mechanics in the epoch were very naive, but for those times they were progressive, for they were an attempt at scientific interpretation of life phenomena. The discovery and research of electrical phenomena in the eighteenth century introduced the idea of "animal electricity" as the main regulator of life. Galvani discovered electric stimulation of muscular contraction and came to the important conclusion that animal and machine electricity are identical. Those and other discoveries developed the understanding of the unity of physical processes in living and nonliving bodies. Lomonosov wrote that "Physiologists must give the causes of the motion of a living body from physics."

In 1780, Lavoisier established the unity of burning and respiration, and in 1828 Wöhler synthesized a substance of living origin—urea—from inorganic substances. The chemistry of life began to unite with general chemistry.

In the nineteenth century, the foundation of scientific biology was laid: Darwin proposed the theory of evolution and Mendel discovered the fundamental laws of genetics. The investigation of biological phenomena had a powerful impact on physics. The law of conservation of energy was discovered by Mayer and Helmholtz, who investigated physiological and medical problems. In 1841, Mayer directed his attention to the fact that the color of the venous blood of people living in the tropics is as bright as that of the arterial blood. He concluded that when the temperature of the environment rises, less energy is necessary for the maintenance of constant body temperature, and he came to formulate the general law of energy conservation and to estimate the mechanical equivalent of heat. Helmholtz considered vitalism, according to which life phenomena are determined by some *vis vitalis* that is inaccessible for scientific cognition, as attributing the features of *perpetuum mobile* to the organism. He formulated the problem of constructing a physics based on the impossibility of existence of perpetual motion, and solved this problem by formulating the law of conservation of energy

(1847). At the end of the nineteenth century, the validity of the law of conservation of energy expressed as the first law of thermodynamics was confirmed for living organisms by direct quantitative experiments. We may say with some exaggeration that if physics gave biology the microscope, biology gave physics the law of conservation of energy.

Boltzmann, founder of statistical mechanics, called the nineteenth century the century of Darwin and studied the mechanical basis of evolution of a physical system. This evolution is described by the second law of thermodynamics, according to which an isolated physical system evolves toward the equilibrium state characterized by the maximal disorder (entropy).

In the second half of the nineteenth century and in the beginning of the twentieth, a set of physical investigations of physiological processes was performed. In particular, Helmholtz studied vision, hearing, and muscular contraction on a physical basis; he was the first to measure the velocity of propagation of the nervous impulse. In 1902, Bernstein discovered biopotentials and established the ionic nature of nervous excitation. One of the first to give a molecular–physical interpretation of heredity was Koltsov (1928) [6], who suggested the first molecular model of the gene. Bauer was the first to suggest a thermodynamic interpretation of life: life is a set of processes that take place in an open nonequilibrium system [7]. Later on, the thermodynamics of biological phenomena was developed in the works of Bertalanffy, Onsager, Prigogine, and others. In 1930, Volterra carried out a mathematical analysis of the so-called "predator–prey" model of the interaction of animal populations [8]. This work is the basis of contemporary physicomathematical modeling of biological processes. We shall speak about biological thermodynamics and mathematical models in the last chapters of this book.

In 1935, Delbrück, Tymofeev-Resovski, and Zimmer discovered the physical nature of mutations. In 1945, Schrödinger, one of the creators of quantum mechanics, published his classic *What is Life? The Physical Aspect of the Living Cell* [9], a book which played a great role in the development of molecular biology and biophysics. Unlike Bohr, Schrödinger suggested the possibility of a general physical interpretation of life phenomena. He formulated a few fundamental physical questions and gave clear answers to some of them. The other questions were answered by molecular biology later on.

The first important question discussed by Schrödinger was How is the nonequilibrium state of the organism maintained? The answer he gave is that the state is maintained by an outflow of entropy from the organism to the surrounding medium.

The second question is Why are atoms small? First, however, we must ask, What does it mean that they are small? In comparison with what are they small? The answer is that atoms are small in comparison with the dimensions of the body of the man; man and the smallest cell consist of a very great number of atoms. Therefore the question may be formulated differently: Why must the organism consist of a great number of atoms? Schrödinger answers: It is because a system consisting of the small number of atoms cannot be ordered; its order would be violated by the accidental fluctuations of thermal motion.

The third question is How can we explain the high stability of the gene, the molecules of hereditary substance built by the light atoms C, H, N, O, P? The hereditary characteristics and the constancy of the biological species are preserved for a great number of generations. Molecular biology, with the help of physics, answered this question, for it discovered the molecular structure and properties of genes, that is, the molecules of deoxyribonucleic acid (DNA).

This extremely short description of the history of biophysics brings us to its modern state, to which this book is devoted.

Nowadays biological physics is developing on a wide front. It is usually divided in three parts:

(1) molecular biophysics, which studies the structure and properties of biologically functional substances and the complexes built by them;

(2) biophysics of the cell, which studies overmolecular, cellular, and subcellular systems; and

(3) biophysics of complicated systems, which deals mainly with physicomathematical modeling of biological processes in cells in the physiological systems of the organisms, in the organisms, in the populations, and in the biosphere as a whole.

The most general problems of biological thermodynamics, information theory, and the physical theory of biological development are connected with the biophysics of complicated systems.

This book follows the above sequence. We begin with molecular biophysics and end with a discussion of general questions.

CHAPTER 2

Physics and Chemistry

Before we direct our attention to the biologically functional substances, we must consider the physical basis of theoretical chemistry. All life processes of the cell or of the organism are determined by chemical reactions, that is, the interactions of big and small molecules and ions. It is impossible to build biophysics without chemistry.

It is not necessary to describe modern theoretical chemistry here, for it has been done in a great number of popular books (see, for example, [4]). We shall emphasize only some concepts that are necessary for the understanding of molecular biophysics.

Classical chemistry distinguishes the simple and multiple valence bonds that are represented, respectively, by one, two, or three valence lines

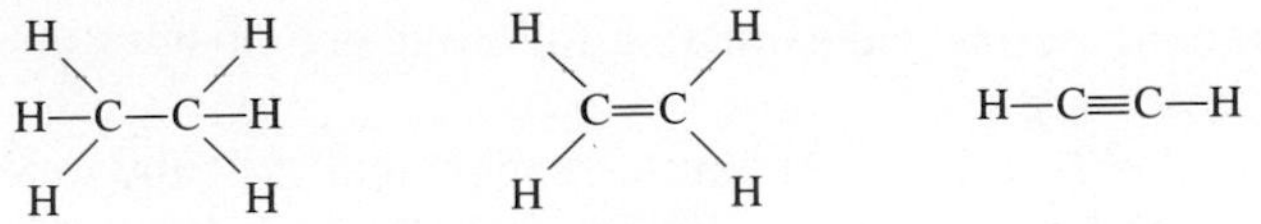

```
 H     H         H     H
  \   /           \   /
H—C—C—H            C=C            H—C≡C—H
  /   \           /   \
 H     H         H     H
  Ethane         Ethylene          Acetylene
```

In chemistry, these structural formulas are well argumented by the reactions of saturation of multiple bonds. For example, in the process of bromination of ethylene, the second bond between the carbon atoms is broken and a saturated compound formed.

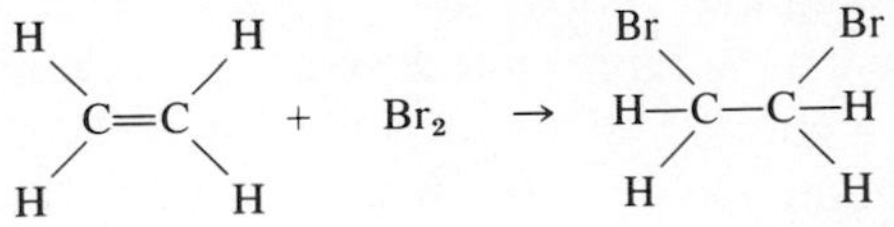

```
 H     H                   Br     Br
  \   /                     \   /
   C=C     +    Br₂   →    H—C—C—H
  /   \                     /   \
 H     H                   H     H
 Ethylene      Bromine    1,2-Dibromoethane
```

What does this mean from the physical point of view? Atoms, which form molecules, are built from atomic nuclei (which, in turn, consist of protons and neutrons) and the electrons that surround them. Quantum mechanics makes it possible to determine the energy states of electrons in the atom. These states are discrete—electrons in an atom can have not all but only some determined levels of energy (as we discuss at the end of this chapter). When a covalent bond is formed, the outer electrons of the interacting atoms are shared by those atoms. In the simplest case of the hydrogen molecule, only two electrons form the chemical bond. The hydrogen molecule can be represented schematically

$$H:H$$

Thus an electron pair corresponds to a valence line. If we know the number of outer electrons in the atom that possess the highest energy, we can determine the valence of the atom. For example, nitrogen has three outer electrons, so its valence is three. Quantum mechanics calculates all the characteristics of the chemical bonds: the energy (that is, the work necessary for breaking the bond), the length of the bond (that is, the distance between the nuclei of the atoms linked by the bond), and the geometrical disposition of the bonds. These calculations are now very precise, and they coincide very well with experiment in the case of simple molecules.

The power of classical chemistry must be emphasized. Long before the creation of quantum mechanics and the development of the physical methods that allow us to analyze quantitatively the structure of molecules (for example, x-ray analysis and spectroscopical methods), chemistry discovered the structural formulas of a multitude of compounds and came to qualitative conclusions about their spatial structures.

From the results of quantum-mechanical calculations and of physics experiments, we know now that the four valence bonds of carbon in its saturated compounds are placed at tetrahedral angles, that the length of the C—C bond is 1.54 Å ($1 \text{ Å} = 10^{-8}$ cm), and that the length of the C—H bond is 1.08 Å. The energy of the C—C bond is 83 kcal/mole, and of the C—H bond 101 kcal/mole.

Figure 1 shows the spatial structure of the ethane molecule.

According to quantum mechanics, the states of the electron in an atom or molecule can be represented by the so-called electron cloud, the density of which, at a given region of space, characterizes the probability of finding the electron in this region. The electron cloud of the hydrogen atom is spherical, and the cloud of the hydrogen

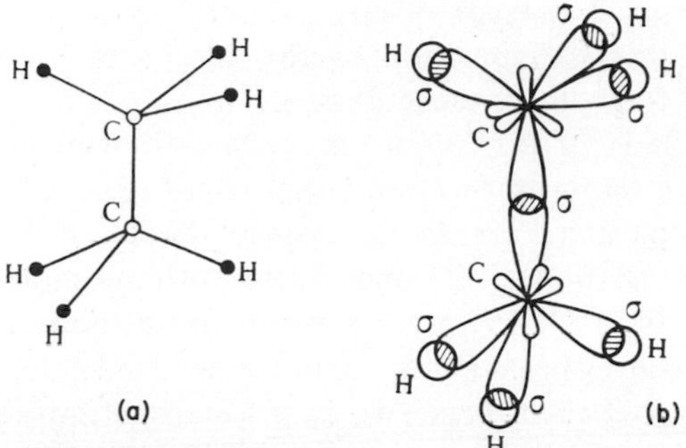

Fig. 1 The structure of the ethane molecule: (a) the valence bonds and (b) the corresponding electronic clouds (σ are single bonds).

molecule is elongated with the maximum density of the cloud in the center of the bond. In Fig. 1, the forms of the electronic clouds of interacting atoms are shown. In the regions of the overlapping of clouds, the electronic density is maximal.

Nonsaturated carbon compounds are formed in another way. The second valence bond in ethylene and the second and third bonds in acetylene are formed by the so-called π-electrons. The maximum of the electronic density of the π-bond appears not at the valence line itself, but above and below it, because the clouds of the π-bonds are situated perpendicular to the bond (Fig. 2). The arrangement of the atoms neighboring the double bonds is planar, that is, all six atoms of ethylene are situated in one plane, and its valence bonds form angles close to 120°. The energy of the second π-bond is less than the energy of the single bond, called the σ-bond. The distance between the atoms linked by the double bond is also smaller. In ethylene, for example, the energy of the double bond is 122 kcal/mole, which is less than the double energy of a single bond, and the length of the C═C bond is 1.34 Å.

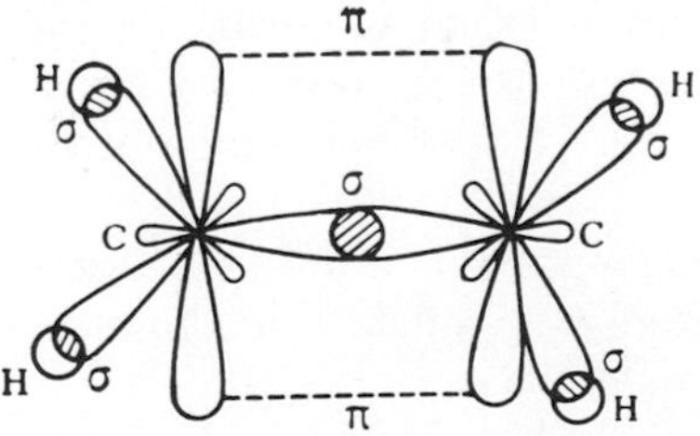

Fig. 2 The structure of the ethylene molecule: σ, single bonds; π, second bond formed by π-electrons.

The triple bond consists of one σ-bond and two π-bonds. It determines the linear disposition of the atoms in the molecule. In acetylene, all four atoms are collinear.

The so-called conformational properties of simple and multiple bonds are very important to biology. From Fig. 1, it is evident that the CH_3 groups can be rotated around the C—C axis in ethane without breaking the C—C bond. In the ethane molecule, internal rotation is possible. On the other hand, turning about the C=C bond in ethylene requires breaking the π-bond, as can be seen from Fig. 2. The difference between these two cases is quantitative. On account of nonvalent interactions between the hydrogen atoms of two CH_3-groups of ethane (we shall speak about nonvalent, weak interactions later), the internal rotation is not completely free. Turning from one state toward another equivalent to the first one, that is, rotating by 120°, requires about 3 kcal/mole of energy. Breaking the π-bond, on the other hand, means breaking a chemical bond and requires approximately 40 kcal/mole of energy.

If the molecule where the internal rotation around a single bond occurs is nonsymmetrical, in contrast to ethane, the turns produce nonequivalent conformations. An example of these conformations, the rotamers of dibromoethane, is shown in Fig. 3. Their existence

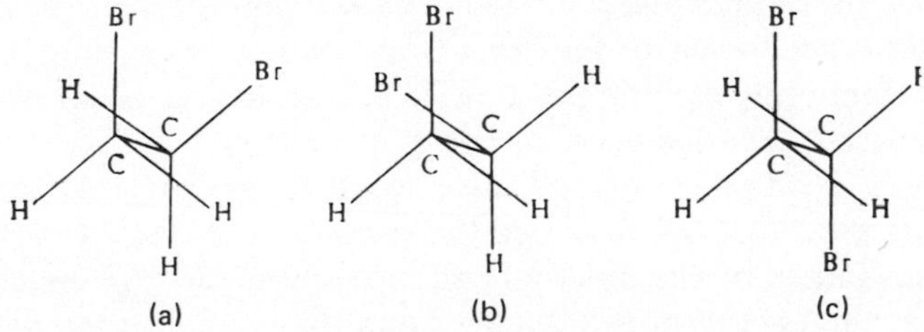

Fig. 3 Rotamers (conformers) of 1,2-dibromoethane: (a) and (b), *gauche* rotamers; (c), *trans* rotamer.

is proved by direct physical experiments, in particular spectroscopic ones. As we shall see, conformations and conformational motility determine the most important properties of biopolymers and polymers.

If in a short or a long chain built by the atoms of carbon, nitrogen, etc., there are alternating single and double bonds (called conjugated bonds), for example

$$H_2C{=}CH{-}CH{=}CH_2$$

$$H_2C{=}CH{-}CH{=}NH$$

then these conjugated chains possess specific electronic properties. The π-electrons in the conjugated chains (or in rings, for example, in benzene) possess motility, that is, they can move along the conjugated chain. This can be seen from many properties of that kind of molecules, in particular from their spectra. Quantum mechanics gives a quantitative explanation of these properties. Let us present a very rough, simple quantum-mechanical calculation of the absorption spectrum of a conjugated chain. If the chain consists of N double and N single alternating bonds, its length is equal to

$$L = Nl, \tag{2}$$

where l is the length of the group C═C—C. Each group of that kind has two π-electrons, and the total number of π-electrons in the chain is $2N$. Let us suggest that π-electrons can move quite freely along the chain, like conduction electrons in a metal. Thus we introduce the metallic model of the molecule. Now we need great energy to remove an electron from the chain. Thus the π-electrons inside the chain have kinetic energy only, and those on its ends have a very high potential energy (practically infinity). The electrons are in a rectangular "potential well" with infinitely high walls (Fig. 4). Let us make an elementary quantum-mechanical calculation of the energy levels of π-electrons in the potential well. According to quantum mechanics, an electron moving with velocity v corresponds to a wave of length

$$\lambda = \frac{h}{mv} \tag{3}$$

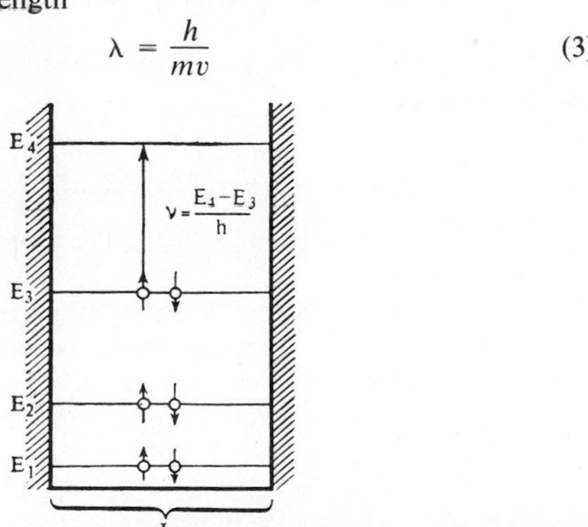

Fig. 4 The potential well for the π-electrons in a chain of conjugated bonds. The energy levels are shown, as is the transition corresponding to the absorption band for the longest wave. The electrons are represented by arrows symbolizing their spins.

where m is the mass of an electron and h is Planck's constant. This is the de Broglie formula. The wave cannot pass through the borders of the well, so the electron cannot leave. In other words, standing waves appear with knots at the walls of the well. In this way, the system is similar to a vibrating string with fixed ends. Possible lengths of the standing waves on a string of length L are

$$\lambda = \frac{2L}{n} \tag{4}$$

where $n = 1, 2, 3, \ldots$. Putting expression (4) in formula (3), we find the possible values of the velocity of the electron:

$$\begin{aligned} v &= \frac{h}{m\lambda} \\ &= \frac{nh}{2mL} \end{aligned} \tag{5}$$

As we have said above, inside the molecule that is modeled by the well, the total energy equals the kinetic energy,

$$E = \frac{mv^2}{2} \tag{6}$$

and, according to (5),

$$E_n = \frac{n^2h^2}{8mL^2}. \tag{7}$$

Thus the energy of the π-electron in the molecule is quantized. It can be equal to

$$\frac{h^2}{8mL^2}, \quad \frac{4h^2}{8mL^2}, \quad \frac{9h^2}{8mL^2}, \quad \ldots$$

but not to any intermediate values. The permitted levels of energy are shown in Fig. 4.

According to quantum mechanics (the Pauli principle [2, 4]), at every level of energy there can be two electrons with antiparallel moments of impulse (spins). Therefore, $2N$ π-electrons of the chain consisting of N links occupy N levels with energies from $h^2/8mL^2$ up to $N^2h^2/8mL^2$. Let us calculate now the frequency ν of the absorption band with the longest wavelength. This frequency corresponds to the transition of the electron from the last occupied level to the first free one.

$$\nu = \frac{1}{h}(E_{N+1} - E_N) \tag{8}$$

We get, according to (7),

$$\nu = \frac{1}{h}\left\{\frac{(N+1)^2h^2}{8mL^2} - \frac{N^2h^2}{8mL^2}\right\} \tag{9}$$

and putting $L = Nl$, we get

$$\nu = \frac{2N+1}{N^2}\frac{h}{8ml^2} \tag{10}$$

If N is big and it is possible to neglect unity in comparison with N, then

$$\nu \cong \frac{h}{4ml^2}\frac{1}{N} \tag{11}$$

that is, the wavelength Λ of the absorption band is proportional to N:

$$\begin{aligned}\Lambda &= \frac{c}{\nu}\\ &\cong \frac{4mcl^2}{h}N \end{aligned} \tag{12}$$

where c is the velocity of light. This means that with the elongation of the conjugated chain, its absorption band shifts toward the longer wavelengths. Formula (12) is confirmed by experiment. Chains that already have six or seven conjugated bonds absorb the light in the visible region; the corresponding substances are dyed. Organic dyes are always conjugated systems.

As the result of the existence of motile π-electrons, the conjugated chain has a planar structure as ethylene does. There is no internal rotation in the chain, and the chain does not have conformational flexibility.

The polymers built by conjugated bonds are always colored, and in some cases they possess semiconductive properties determined by the motility of π-electrons.

CHAPTER 3

Some Properties of Electron Waves

The treatment of the behavior of π-electrons that are free inside the potential well allows us to get a simple and clear explanation of the color of the molecules of organic substances. Furthermore, these results help us to understand some properties of biopolymers—proteins and nucleic acids.

Speaking of the potential well model, it is difficult to resist the temptation of examining it in greater detail. In this chapter we shall digress a little from the main theme of the book, but the simple investigation given here will be useful for some biophysical problems.

As we have already seen, the model of the potential well allows us to obtain the energy levels and the spectrum of the system without solving the Schrödinger equation. In the given case, the solution is quite rigorous. We can ask whether it is possible with the help of the model of this type to solve other problems of quantum mechanics. The answer is yes.

Let us consider the quantization of the harmonic oscillator. A particle is under the action of the elastic force $f = -kx$ that is proportional to the displacement x of the particle from its equilibrium position and that tends to return the particle to this position. Evidently, the particle will perform harmonic oscillations. Let us find their frequency. According to Newton's second law,

$$m \frac{d^2x}{dt^2} = f = -kx, \tag{13}$$

where m is the mass of the particle and d^2x/dt^2, the second derivative of displacement x by time t, is the acceleration. Let us look for the solution of Eq. (13) in the form

$$x = x_0 \cos 2\pi\nu t \tag{14}$$

We get $d^2x/dt^2 = -x_0 4\pi^2\nu^2 \cos 2\pi\nu t$. Putting these values of x and d^2x/dt^2 in (13), we find the frequency ν of oscillations:

$$\nu = \frac{1}{2\pi}\sqrt{\frac{k}{m}} \tag{15}$$

The energy E of the oscillator is the sum of the kinetic and potential energies:

$$E = \frac{kx^2}{2} + \frac{mv^2}{2} \tag{16}$$

where v is the velocity of the particle. The graph of the potential energy of the oscillator is the parabola $kx^2/2$ (Fig. 5). The microparticle, oscillating with amplitude x_0, moves in a segment of length $2x_0$, and the velocity of this motion is not constant; it depends on the coordinate x. At points $x = \pm x_0$, the velocity is equal to zero as it changes sign. Thus, as the energy E is constant,

$$\frac{kx^2}{2} + \frac{mv^2}{2} = \frac{kx_0^2}{2}$$

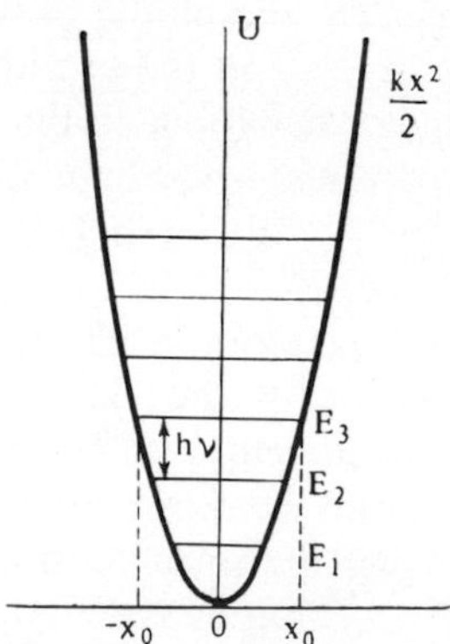

Fig. 5 The potential well for the harmonic oscillator and the calculated energy levels.

and

$$v = \sqrt{\frac{k}{m}(x_0^2 - x^2)}$$
$$= 2\pi\nu\sqrt{x_0^2 - x^2}$$

So the length of the de Broglie wave corresponding to the motion of the oscillator, $\lambda = h/mv$, is also not constant. Let us now make a nonrigorous assumption: we shall suppose that the total energy of the particle is equal to its kinetic energy in the whole segment from the point x_0 to $-x_0$. In other words, we consider the oscillator as a free particle in a parabolic potential well. On the walls of the well, the total energy is equal to the potential energy, that is,

$$E = \frac{kx_0^2}{2}$$

Therefore the distance between the walls is

$$L = 2x_0 = 2\sqrt{\frac{2E}{k}} \tag{17}$$

Assuming that inside the well on the whole segment L the kinetic energy remains constant, that is,

$$\frac{mv^2}{2} = \frac{kx_0^2}{2}$$

we suppose that the velocity of the particle inside the well is constant, too. The particle of that kind corresponds to standing de Broglie waves with wavelengths determined by the condition [compare Eq. (4)]

$$\lambda_n = \frac{2L}{n}$$
$$= \frac{4}{n}\sqrt{\frac{2E_n}{k}} \tag{18}$$

Thus the possible values of the velocity of the particle are

$$v_n = \frac{h}{m\lambda_n}$$
$$= \frac{nh}{4m}\sqrt{\frac{k}{2E_n}} \tag{19}$$

and the energy of the oscillator is found from the condition

$$E_n = \frac{mv_n^2}{2}$$

$$= \frac{m}{2}\left(\frac{nh}{4m}\sqrt{\frac{k}{2E_n}}\right)^2 \tag{20}$$

Solving Eq. (20), we get

$$E_n = \frac{nh}{8}\sqrt{\frac{k}{m}} \tag{21}$$

or, taking into account expression (15),

$$E_n = \frac{2\pi n}{8} h\nu$$

$$= \frac{\pi}{4} nh\nu \tag{22}$$

where $n = 0,1,2, \ldots$.

The rigorous solution of the problem, with the help of the Schrödinger equation, is

$$E_n = \frac{h\nu}{2} + nh\nu, \qquad n = 0,1,2 \ldots \tag{23}$$

The nonrigorous solution (22) is similar to the rigorous solution (23): the energy levels of the oscillator are equidistant and the distance between neighboring levels is constant. In solution (22), the distance between neighboring levels is

$$E_{n+1} - E_n = \frac{\pi}{4} h\nu$$

In the strict solution,

$$E_{n+1} - E_n = h\nu$$

There is a difference in the numeral multiplier, but the law of quantization is reproduced well. Moreover, according to the rigorous solution, the minimum energy of the harmonic oscillator at $n = 0$ differs from zero and is equal to $h\nu/2$. In our nonrigorous solution, it is zero.

Let us consider another problem: the quantization of the hydrogen atom. The electron potential energy U caused by the interaction with the nucleus is

$$U = -\frac{e^2}{r} \tag{24}$$

where e is the charge of the electron, and r the distance between the nucleus and the electron. The potential energy is negative because work must be done to bring the electron away from the pull of the nucleus. The curve (24) is hyperbolic (Fig. 6). It is possible to assume that at a given value of r, the electron moves in the atom inside a region with linear size r.

Let us perform another nonrigorous calculation based on the consideration of standing waves. We shall assume that the electron energy is equal to its potential energy at the boundary of the mentioned region, that is, on the hyperbola

$$\begin{aligned} E &= U \\ &= -\frac{e^2}{r} \end{aligned}$$

Inside the segment, the energy of the electron on each point x is the sum of the kinetic and potential energy; but we shall assume as before that inside the well with hyperbolic walls the electron is free, that is, the total energy equals the kinetic one

$$\begin{aligned} -E &= \frac{mv^2}{r} \\ &= \frac{e^2}{r} \end{aligned} \tag{25}$$

We get from (25)

$$\begin{aligned} v &= \sqrt{-\frac{2E}{m}} \\ &= \sqrt{\frac{2e^2}{mr}} \end{aligned} \tag{26}$$

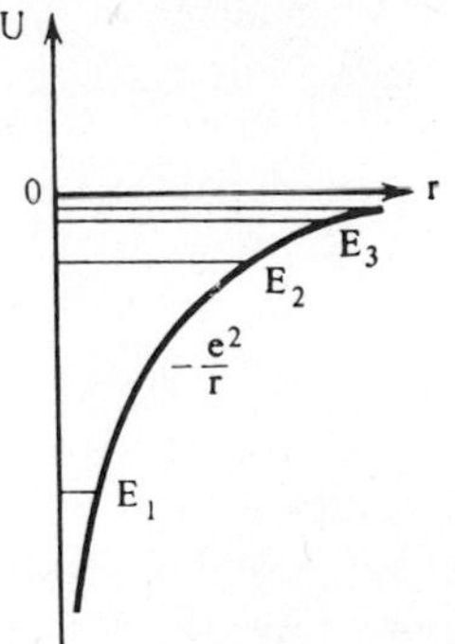

Fig. 6 The potential well for the hydrogen atom, and the calculated energy levels.

The lengths of the standing de Broglie waves are

$$\lambda_n = \frac{2r}{n}$$
$$= -\frac{2e^2}{nE_n} \tag{27}$$

Hence, the possible values of the velocity of electron are

$$v_n = \frac{h}{m\lambda_n}$$
$$= -\frac{nhE_n}{2me^2} \tag{28}$$

and we obtain the values of the energy from the condition

$$-E_n = \frac{mv_n^2}{2}$$
$$= \frac{n^2h^2E_n^2}{8me^4} \tag{29}$$

We get

$$E_n = -\frac{8me^4}{n^2h^2}, \qquad n = 1,2,3, \ldots \tag{30}$$

The rigorous solution of the Schrödinger equation for this problem is

$$E_n = -\frac{2\pi^2me^4}{n^2h^2}, \qquad n = 1,2,3, \ldots \tag{31}$$

Solutions (30) and (31) differ from each other only by a numerical factor. A nonrigorous, visual solution rightly reproduces the law of quantization. The levels of energy in the atom converge as the quantum number n increases. The ratios of the energies at consecutive levels are

$$E_1 : E_2 : E_3 : \cdots = 1 : \frac{1}{4} : \frac{1}{9} : \cdots$$

If $n \to \infty$, $r \to \infty$, and $E_n \to 0$, the electron is torn off from the atom. The energy of the free electron is positive, and the spectrum of its possible values is continuous.

The similarity of the nonrigorous solutions to the rigorous ones holds for potential functions that are powers of x, and is defined by the so-called virial theorem, according to which the mean kinetic energy is proportional to the mean potential energy.

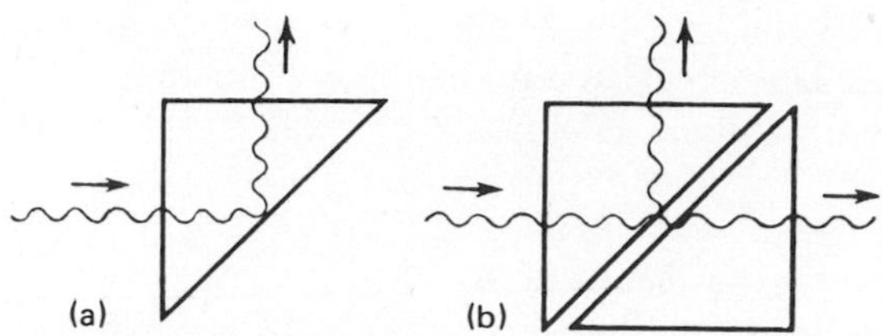

Fig. 7 (a) Total internal reflection prism; and (b) two total internal reflection prisms separated by less than a wavelength.

The visual model of the potential well makes it possible to consider the important notions of quantum mechanics without resorting to complicated solutions of the Schrödinger equation.

In all three cases—in the rectangular, parabolic, and hyperbolic wells—the walls of the well are spread to infinity, and hence the electron wave is totally reflected at the walls of the well. A standing wave with knots on the wall is formed. If the wall of the potential well is not infinitely high and wide, the electron wave can leak through it. This can be seen more clearly with the help of a classical analogy. Let us imagine a total internal reflection prism (Fig. 7a). A light ray does not penetrate the slanting wall, but is reflected by it, changing the direction by 90°. However, if a second prism, identical to the first one, is placed close to it—the separation being of the order of the length of the light wave—the light will penetrate through both prisms (Fig. 7b). This will happen because the light wave penetrates a small distance through the first prism and can move further in the second one. On the basis of this analogy, the theory of α decay of the atomic nucleus was proposed (Gamow). The microparticle—be it the α particle or the electron—can leak through the potential barrier of finite height and width (Fig. 8). The penetration of that kind of microparticle is usually called the tunnel effect. The velocity of the tunneling is independent of temperature.

Among the biochemical processes, there are important pro-

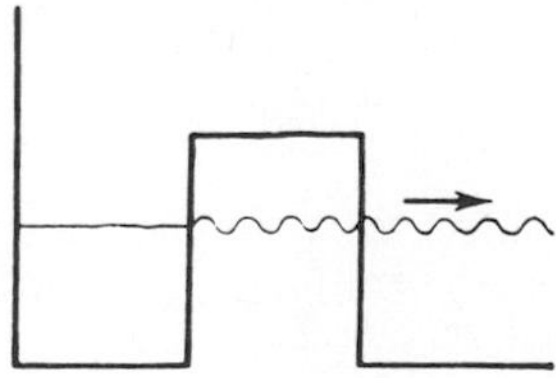

Fig. 8 Transition of a microparticle through a potential barrier.

cesses of electron transfer from one molecule to another; transportation of that kind is realized in the respiration chain, that is, in reactions of the oxidation–reduction type:

$$Fe^{3+} + e^{-} \rightleftarrows Fe^{2+}.$$

(Fe is iron, e^{-} is an electron).

Electron tunneling happens to be possible in processes of this kind.

The probability of the particle's penetration through the barrier decreases with the increase of the particle's mass. Thus in ordinary chemical reactions the molecules do not "penetrate"; they do not tunnel through the barrier, but roll over it. In that case, the velocity of the reaction depends strongly on temperature.

CHAPTER 4

Strong and Weak Interactions of Molecules

Molecules interact with each other; atoms and atomic groups interact inside molecules. We use the term "strong interactions" for chemical interactions, and "weak interactions" for intermolecular and intramolecular interactions that do not lead to transformation of the molecules.

How does a chemical reaction proceed? A chemical reaction is the transformation of the electron clouds of the molecules that take part in strong interactions. This is followed by a change in the arrangement of the atomic nuclei. The reaction will proceed if the necessary thermodynamic and kinetic conditions are fulfilled. The necessary thermodynamic condition is that the free energy of the products of reaction be smaller than the free energy of the reagents. Free energy is the quantity

$$G = H - TS \tag{32}$$

where T is the absolute temperature, S the entropy, and H the enthalpy, given by

$$H = E + pV \tag{33}$$

where E is internal energy, p the pressure, and V the volume. If

$$G_{\text{products}} < G_{\text{reagents}} \tag{34}$$

the reaction is possible. In the opposite case, the reaction cannot proceed by itself. Condition (34) is necessary, but is not yet sufficient. The reaction may be possible in principle, but its rate may be so small that the reaction will not proceed. The fulfillment of kinetic conditions is also necessary. In most cases, this boils down to the requirement that the reagents possess surplus energy (energy of activation) in order for the reaction to proceed. Evidently, the greater the energy of the system, the faster and easier an electron transformation will occur because this transformation means the break of some chemical bonds and the formation of others. The energy scheme of the reaction is shown in Fig. 9. The reaction takes place if the system crosses the activation barrier. Hence, the reaction rate depends on the temperature, increasing with an increase in temperature.

Let us consider a very simple reaction in the gaseous phase

$$H_2 + I_2 \rightarrow 2HI$$

where H is hydrogen, and I iodine. The rate of this reaction is

$$v = kC_{H_2}C_{I_2} \tag{35}$$

where C_{H_2}, C_{I_2} are the concentrations of hydrogen and iodine, and k is the rate constant of reaction. According to contemporary physics,

$$\begin{aligned} k &= \frac{RT}{N_A h} \exp\left(-\frac{G_a}{RT}\right) \\ &= \frac{RT}{N_A h} \exp\left(\frac{S_a}{R}\right) \exp\left(-\frac{H_a}{RT}\right) \end{aligned} \tag{36}$$

where R is the gas constant; G_a, S_a, H_a are correspondingly the free energy, entropy, and enthalpy of activation; and N_A is Avogadro's

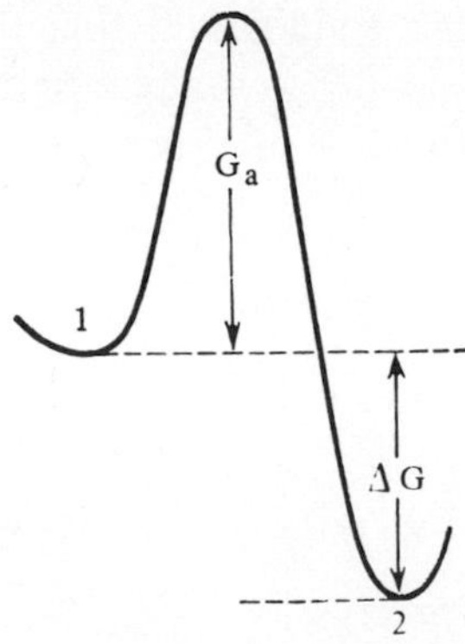

Fig. 9 Energy scheme of a chemical reaction: ΔG is the change of free energy, G_a the free energy of activation.

number. Formula (36) describes the mentioned crossing of the barrier. The higher the temperature, the larger is the amount of thermal energy stored in molecules and the probability for the molecule to possess energy (enthalpy) equal to or larger than the activation enthalpy H_a. Therefore the reaction rate depends very strongly—in fact, exponentially—on temperature.

As is known, a catalyst is a substance in the presence of which the reaction proceeds faster; the catalyst itself leaves the reaction unchanged. Catalytic action depends on the formation of intermediate bonds—strong or weak—between the reagents and the catalyst. No catalyst can provide a reaction that does not satisfy condition (34). The catalyst does not influence the difference of the free energies of the initial and final states of the reacting system, but only the height of the barrier that separates these two states. The role of the catalyst is only to lower the free energy of activation, and thereby accelerate the reaction. In biology, all this is very important, as all biological processes are catalytic, with the role of the catalysts being played by special proteins—the enzymes.

As we shall see, in an open system, which exchanges substance and energy with the surrounding medium (and biological systems are of just this kind), the catalyst can influence not only the rate of the process, but the difference of the free energies of the initial and final states as well.

Let us consider now nonvalent, weak interactions among the molecules and inside them. An understanding of the nature of these interactions is necessary in molecular biophysics.

All kinds of gases liquefy at sufficiently low temperature and sufficiently high pressure. This means that there are forces of cohesion among the gas molecules. These forces are not chemical, as the chemical bonds are already saturated inside the molecule. The energy of the intermolecular interaction is much lower than the energy of the chemical bonds—the order of its value is lower than 10 kcal/mole, whereas that of chemical bonds is of the order of several tens of kilocalories per mole.

Intermolecular forces are usually called van der Waals forces. Physics provides the possibility of calculating these forces on the basis of quantum mechanics and of explaining, for example, why the inert gases, which consist of chemically noninteracting molecules, liquefy. The van der Waals forces decrease rapidly with increasing intermolecular distance r, depending on it as r^{-7}, and correspondingly the energy of intermolecular attraction is proportional to r^{-6}.

If the molecules possess an asymmetric distribution of electric charges (for example, in the molecule HCl, the positive charge is shifted toward the atom H, the negative one toward the atom Cl), then ordinary electrostatics makes its contribution to the van der Waals forces; orientational and inductional effects are determined by the attraction of charges of opposite sign and repulsion of charges of like sign. Interactions among the ions (charged molecules and atoms) occur in accordance with Coulomb's law. A detailed description of intermolecular forces is given in many books (for example, [10]).

At small distances, atoms that do not form chemical bonds do not attract, but repel each other. Quantum mechanics explains the nature of this repulsion as the impossibility of squeezing two electronic systems into each other. The total potential energy of interaction of two molecules, where the chemical bonds are already saturated, can be described by various formulas, for example,

$$U = \frac{A}{r^{12}} - \frac{B}{r^6} \tag{37}$$

The first term describes the repulsion, the second one the van der Waals attraction. The form of this function is shown in Fig. 10.

A similar interaction—but this time intramolecular—determines the existence of rotational isomerism, found in conformers or rotamers. The molecule possesses the conformation corresponding to the minimal energy of all weak interactions. For dibromoethane, the rotamers shown in Fig. 3 have smaller energy than the molecules with other angles of rotation around the C—C bond, the energy of rotamer 3 is the minimal one, and the energies of rotamers 1 and 2 are equal and higher than the energy of the trans rotamer 3. This is shown in Fig. 11, where the curve of dependence of the energy of the $BrH_2C—CH_2Br$ molecule on the angle of rotation φ around the C—C bond is presented.

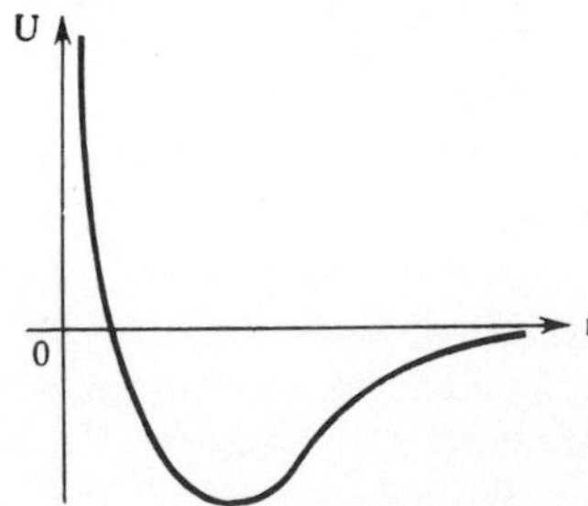

Fig. 10 Potential function expressing intermolecular interaction.

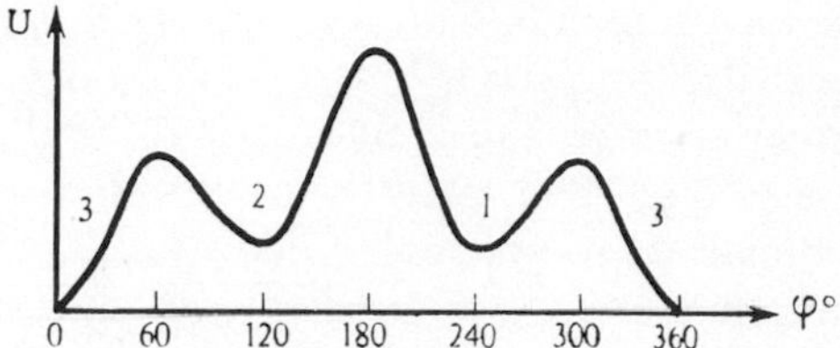

Fig. 11 Potential energy curve for internal rotation in dibromoethane: 1 and 2, *gauche* rotamers; 3, *trans* rotamer.

The so-called hydrogen bonds play a very important role in biology. The atoms of hydrogen, connected with oxygen, nitrogen, phosphorus, and fluorine (but as a rule not with carbon) can form additional chemical bonds with the same atoms of this or other molecules. Thus, for example, the molecules of formic acid (even in vapor) form dimers at the expense of hydrogen bonds (dotted lines)

```
        O · · · H—O
      //           \
  H—C               C—H
      \            //
        O—H · · · O
```

The hydrogen bonds are determined by the possibility of the smallest atom—hydrogen—penetrating the electronic shells of the bonded atoms to tighten them. The distance between the atoms O in the group O—H · · · O, is 2.55 Å, less than the sum of two atomic radii of oxygen—2.80 Å. The energy of the hydrogen bond is 4–7 kcal/mole, which is of the same order as the energy of intermolecular interaction. The physical theory gives the explanation of the hydrogen bond, and its quantitative characteristics in accordance with experiment.

The existence of hydrogen bonds explains the peculiar features of water, in particular, the stability of its liquid state in a broad interval of 100°. As shown in Fig. 12, each H_2O molecule in ice is

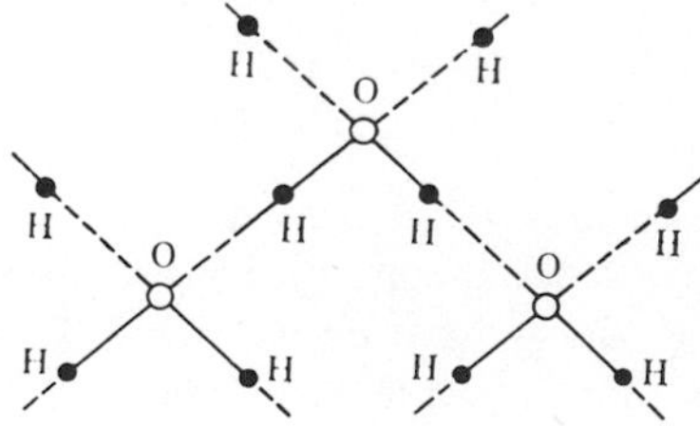

Fig. 12 Hydrogen bonds connecting H_2O molecules.

connected by hydrogen bonds with four others in a tetrahedral arrangement. The structure of ice is loose—only four neighbors of the molecule is a comparatively small number. In the liquid state, this regular structure is disturbed; side by side with molecules having four hydrogen bonds there are molecules with three, two, or one hydrogen bond, and there are molecules without hydrogen bonds. Liquid water is packed more densely than ice. At normal pressure, the density of water is maximum not at 0°C, but at 4°C. Roughly speaking we can consider water to be a mixture of the loose but regular structure of ice and a compactly packed but irregular structure [10].

The solubility of various substances in water is determined by peculiarities of its structure. In water, electrolytes—salts, bases, and acids—are highly soluble because of the high dielectric permeability of water. The electrolytes dissociate into ions in aqueous solution. In water, substances with big dipole moments are soluble, as are substances, such as ethyl alcohol, that are able to form hydrogen bonds with the water molecules. Alcohol is characterized by formation of complexes of the type

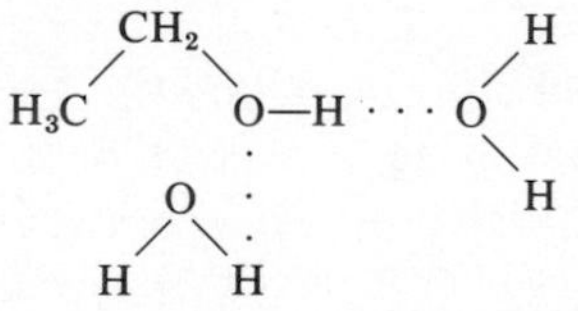

```
       CH2              H
      /   \            /
  H3C      O—H · · · O
           ·          \
       O   ·           H
      / \  ·
     H   H
```

This is what provides the strength of alcoholic beverages. On the other hand, the hydrocarbons (such as benzene, C_6H_6) are practically insoluble in water. Gasoline, which is a mixture of hydrocarbons, separates from water. The same occurs with fats and oils, whose molecules contain long hydrocarbon chains. This means that

$$H_2O \cdots H_2O \qquad C_6H_6 \cdots C_6H_6$$

contacts are more advantageous than

$$H_2O \cdots C_6H_6 \qquad C_6H_6 \cdots H_2O$$

contacts. What does it mean that they are advantageous? Solubility in the thermodynamic sense means that the free energy of solution is smaller than the free energy of water and solute taken separately; if the substance does not dissolve, the solution increases the free energy. This increase can have two causes. As the difference of free energies of the initial substances and the solution is equal to

$$G_{\text{initial}} - G_{\text{solution}} = \Delta G = \Delta H - T\Delta S \tag{38}$$

$\Delta G < 0$, which means that the substance will not dissolve, if $\Delta H < 0$, $\Delta S < 0$ when $|\Delta H| > T|\Delta S|$; $\Delta H > 0$ and $\Delta S > 0$, while $|\Delta H| < T|\Delta S|$; or last, if $\Delta H < 0$ and $\Delta S > 0$ simultaneously.

Experiment shows that during the interaction of hydrocarbon with water, $\Delta S > 0$ and $\Delta H > 0$, but $\Delta H < T\,\Delta S$.

The insolubility is determined by the lowering of entropy in solution. This follows from the fact that if the temperature increases, the small solubility of hydrocarbons in water becomes even smaller. Hence, the water that surrounds the molecule of the hydrocarbon obtains a more regular structure. As the effect is entropic and not energetic, the pushing out of the molecules of hydrocarbon from water must be considered as a result of these specific interactions, which are called hydrophobic. The theory makes calculation of these interactions possible.

We have considered some questions in chemistry and molecular physics, a field that has been shaped by the powerful development of quantum and statistical mechanics in our century. Fifty years ago, the first quantitative theory of the chemical bond was developed and the calculation for the simplest molecule, H_2, performed. Today we possess the tools for calculating theoretically all quantitative characteristics of rather complicated molecules—energy; bond lengths; angles between the bonds; electrical, optical, and spectral constants; distribution of electronic density; and finally, chemical reactivity. These calculations are, however, very complicated and bulky; they require vast amounts of computer time. At the same time, we cannot say that all the problems of theoretical chemistry are solved. In particular, big difficulties remain in the theoretical investigation of chemical reactions in the liquid phase; formula (36) is valid only for gas phase. Nevertheless, the principal solutions of the main problems of chemistry are obtained from physics. In this sense, physics and chemistry are already united.

Of course chemistry not only maintained its importance and independence, but even developed further. Today chemical reactions are investigated first of all with the help of chemical methods. Although the reactions can be analyzed through mathematical calculations, it is not expedient to substitute calculations for chemical methods, which can solve the problems much faster and more effectively. The situation is similar to that in radioelectronics. Although it is known that any electrotechnical or radiotechnical system obeys the laws of electrodynamics, that is, of theoretical physics, these laws are not used in calculating complicated electrotechnical networks. Much more simple and convenient methods for obtaining these goals have been developed in electrotechnics and radiotechnics.

Henceforth, when speaking about physics in biology, we shall mean physics and chemistry in biology, as the theoretical fundamentals of chemistry belong to physics.

What are the chemical peculiarities of living systems? What chemical and molecular problems do we encounter in the study of life?

The cell is a special chemical machine, in which a number of different chemical reactions, including many very complicated ones, take place. These catalytic reactions proceed in ''soft conditions'' at physiological temperature, at normal pressure, and in aqueous surroundings. Every biochemical reaction needs its specific catalyst. The role of these catalysts is played by the proteins, by enzymes.

A considerable part of biochemical reactions are the biosynthetic reactions, which lead to formation of the substances necessary for life, primarily of the proteins. Not only enzymes, but also nucleic acids and other substances are necessary for these processes.

Various types of work are performed in the cell: energy is spent for biosynthesis, for the transportation of substances inside the cells and outside of them, and for mechanical motion of entire cells and of their organoids. Electric work is also done at the cellular membrane, where a potential difference is created. All these types of work are done at the expense of chemical energy stored in definite substances, the most important of which is adenosine–triphosphorous acid (ATP). The physicochemical mechanisms of ATP synthesis in the cell are known.

The life of the cell is determined by exactly balanced concentrations of biologically functional substances. This system is well regulated in space and time. We have called the cell a chemical machine, meaning that among organoids of the cell and its molecules there are direct connections and feedback. The principal difference between the cell and the machine, the man-made robot, is in the nature of these connections or signals that determine the regulation and management in the living system. In artificial machines, the signalization is electrical, magnetic, or mechanical. In living systems, the signals are molecules and ions; the sources and receivers of signals are molecular structures. The enzyme that catalyzes the conversion of reagent (substrate) into a product can be considered as a transformer of molecular chemical signals.

We can say that chemistry and molecular physics are the fundamentals of the biology of cells and organisms. Life begins at the level of molecules, and it is meaningless to speak of "submolecular biology." Correspondingly, biology deals with electronic and conformational transformations of molecules, but not with transformations of matter at deeper levels, for example, at the level of atomic nuclei.

We can now formulate the main problems of molecular biophysics. However, before that we shall consider the peculiarities of macromolecules, for the main biologically functional substances—proteins and nucleic acids—are macromolecular substances.

CHAPTER 5

The Physics of Macromolecules

In the overwhelming majority of cases, macromolecules are built of long chains containing nonconjugated σ-bonds. Examples are polyethylene

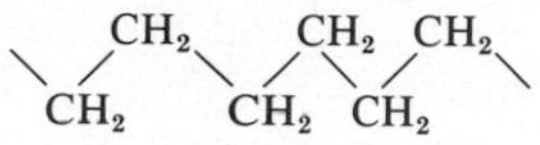

$$\diagdown\underset{CH_2}{\diagup}\overset{CH_2}{}\diagdown\underset{CH_2}{\diagup}\overset{CH_2}{}\diagdown\underset{CH_2}{\diagup}\overset{CH_2}{}\diagdown$$

and natural rubber

$$-H_2C\diagup HC{=}C(CH_3)\diagdown CH_2{-}CH_2\diagup HC{=}C(CH_3)\diagdown CH_2{-}CH_2\diagup$$

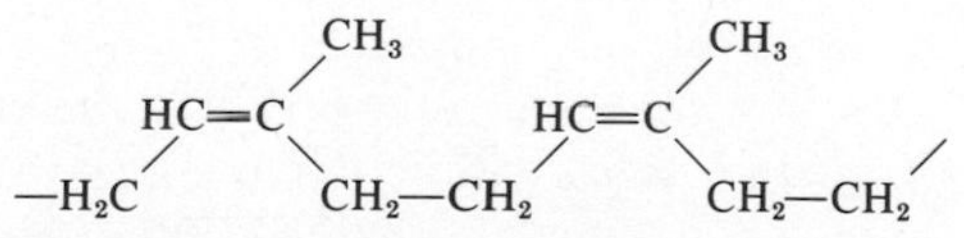

Macromolecules of biopolymers also contain nonconjugated single bonds. Proteins are macromolecules whose links are amino acid residues. Amino acids have the structure

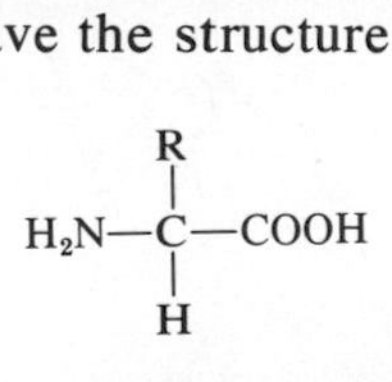

$$H_2N{-}\underset{\displaystyle H}{\overset{\displaystyle R}{\underset{|}{\overset{|}{C}}}}{-}COOH$$

where R indicates various atomic groups. The protein chain is formed by polycondensation of amino acids. In the process of unification of two amino acids, a peptide bond CO—NH is formed and a water molecule removed:

$$H_2N-\overset{\displaystyle R_1}{\underset{\displaystyle H}{\overset{|}{\underset{|}{C}}}}-COOH + H_2N-\overset{\displaystyle R_2}{\underset{\displaystyle H}{\overset{|}{\underset{|}{C}}}}-COOH$$

$$\xrightarrow{-H_2O} H_2N-\overset{\displaystyle R_1}{\underset{\displaystyle H}{\overset{|}{\underset{|}{C}}}}-CO-NH-\overset{\displaystyle R_2}{\underset{\displaystyle H}{\overset{|}{\underset{|}{C}}}}-COOH$$

All proteins in nature are built of twenty kinds of amino acids. In other words, the protein chain is a text written with a twenty letter alphabet. Amino acids differ from one another by the structure of the R groups. These groups contain the atoms C and H, in a series of cases O and N, and in two cases S. In the most simple amino acid, glycine, the R group is H. Structural formulas of 20 canonical amino acids are presented in many books, in particular, [10].

Macromolecules of nucleic acids also contain nonconjugated single bonds in a chain.

Let us consider first the general peculiarities of macromolecules determined by their chain structure. It is clear that without understanding these peculiarities it is impossible to understand molecular biophysics. Without understanding the main properties of rubber, it is impossible to understand enzymatic activity.

As we have seen, internal rotations around single bonds are possible in molecules. The macromolecule of polyethylene in solution (polyethylene is soluble in hydrocarbons) is in a state of thermal motion, during which the turns of atomic groups around single bonds of the chain occur. What will happen to a chain of that sort with rotating links? It will be folded into the coil. Let the chain consist of N links, each of length l. What will be the average distance between the beginning and the end of the chain (Fig. 13)? In average it will be equal to zero, because as the result of thermal motion, the probabil-

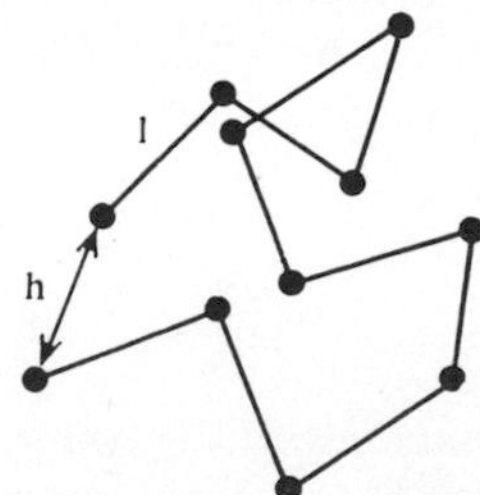

Fig. 13 Coiled polymer chain.

ity that the end of the chain will be found on the right is equal to the probability that it will be found on the left.

The problem of determining the average distance is similar to the problem of Brownian motion. The mean square distance between the ends of the chain is nonzero. If the chain is a free joined one, as shown in Fig. 13, then the mean square distance between the beginning and the end is equal to

$$\overline{h^2} = Nl^2 \tag{39}$$

This value characterizes the size of the polymeric statistical coil. If the chain would be completely stretched, the square of its length would be equal to N^2l^2. In the coil, the square of length diminishes N times, so the length itself diminishes $\sqrt{N}$ times.

The formation of the loose statistical coils by polymers in solution is proved by direct experiments; in particular, the coils are well seen in electron microscopic photographs. The folding of polymer chains into coils explains the main physical peculiarity of polymers—the high elasticity of rubber.

The properties of rubber are rather surprising. Experimental and theoretical investigations of rubber led to the creation of important new fields of physics: polymer physics and molecular biophysics. This is one of the rare cases where scientific investigations were stimulated by the needs of technology. If rubber were not so widely used in the car industry, physics would probably not be so interested in it. The development of biopolymer physics, molecular biophysics, and biology would be slower. In general, however, science develops in accordance with its own logic, independently of technology, and only afterward finds its practical applications. Faraday did not think about the dynamo, and Maxwell and Hertz did not forsee radiotechnology.

What is the high elasticity of rubber? A piece of rubber can be stretched by hundreds of percent with comparatively small effort. The elasticity modulus of rubber is many orders less than the elasticity modulus of metal. Both the rubber tube and the steel wire obey Hooke's law of the proportionality of stress and deformation:

$$p = \varepsilon \frac{L - L_0}{L_0} \tag{40}$$

where L and L_0 are the lengths of the stressed and nonstressed samples, respectively, and ε is the modulus of elasticity. For steel, $\varepsilon \approx$ 20,000 kg/mm^2; for rubber, $\varepsilon =$ 0.02–0.8 kg/mm^2 (depending on the

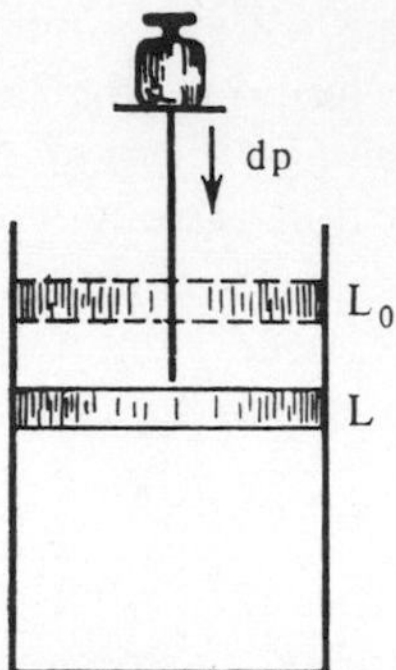

Fig. 14 Compression of the gas in a cylinder by a piston.

degree of vulcanization of the rubber). Such a small modulus of elasticity characterizes an ideal gas. Actually, the ideal gas is described by the Clapeyron equation of state

$$pV = RT \tag{41}$$

where p is pressure, V volume, T absolute temperature, and R the gas constant. Let us compress gas at constant temperature, increasing the pressure by dp (Fig. 14). The volume will diminish by dV. From Eq. (41), we get

$$p\,dV + V\,dp = 0$$

and

$$\begin{aligned} dp &= -p\,\frac{dV}{V} \\ &= p\,\frac{L_0 - L}{L_0} \end{aligned} \tag{42}$$

where L_0 is the initial and L the final position of the piston (Fig. 14). This equation is similar to (40), where the role of the modulus of elasticity is played by the atmospheric pressure p. It is equal to 1 kg/cm^2 = 0.01 kg/mm^2, the value of the same order as ε of rubber.

The similarity of rubber and the ideal gas does not end here. Gas becomes heated during adiabatic compression, as everyone who has pumped a bicycle or an automobile tire knows. The rubber is heating during adiabatic stretching, as one can easily see by quickly stretching a rubber band close to one's lips. This means that in both cases heat is released, and correspondingly the entropy of gas or rubber is reduced. The work done by stretching rubber with the force f by dL

is equal to (compare Chapter 4)

$$\begin{aligned} f\,dL &= dG \\ &= dH - T\,dS \end{aligned} \tag{43}$$

where G is the free energy, H the enthalpy, and S the entropy. It follows from (43) that the elastic force at isothermic stretching of rubber is equal to

$$\begin{aligned} f &= \left(\frac{\partial G}{\partial L}\right)_T \\ &= \left(\frac{\partial H}{\partial L}\right)_T - T\left(\frac{\partial S}{\partial L}\right)_T \end{aligned} \tag{44}$$

The experiment shows that for rubber, the elastic force is proportional to absolute temperature T, and the straight line $f(T)$ comes close to the coordinate origin. This means that in formula (44) the enthalpy (internal energy) of rubber does not depend on the stretching:

$$\left(\frac{\partial H}{\partial L}\right)_T \approx 0 \tag{45}$$

Condition (45) is similar to a known property of the ideal gas: its energy's independence of the occupied volume. From (44) and (45), we obtain that the elastic force in rubber is given by

$$f \approx -T\left(\frac{\partial S}{\partial L}\right)_T \tag{46}$$

and the modulus of elasticity of rubber is proportional to absolute temperature (as for the ideal gas in the formula (42), where

$$p = \left(\frac{RT}{V}\right)$$

The elasticity of rubber and gas depends not on energy but on entropy. During the stretching of rubber or during compression of a gas, the entropy decreases while the energy does not change. On the other hand, during the stretching of a solid body, such as a steel spring, the internal energy increases but the entropy practically does not change.

The entropy dependence of the elasticity of an ideal gas means that when the occupied volume decreases, the frequency of impacts of the molecules at the walls of the vessel increases; the elastic force is determined by the thermal motion of the molecules. The higher is the probability of a given state of the system, that is, the greater is the number of ways of realizing that state, the higher is the entropy of the system. Compression of the gas reduces its entropy as the gas is transferred from the more probable rarefied state into the less probable compressed state. Similarity of the rubber and gas in this sense means only that rubber consists also of a large number of independently moving elements and that the stretching of rubber provides the transition from a more probable distribution of these elements to a less probable distribution.

The links of the polymer chain rotating around the single bonds are these independently moving elements. Macromolecules fold into the coil because this state is more probable and the higher entropy corresponds to it.

Actually, the folded state with the length of chain equal to $\sqrt{\overline{h^2}} = \sqrt{N}l$ can be achieved in many different ways, but a completely stretched chain with length Nl can be obtained only one way.

During the stretching of rubber, the coils are stretched and entropy diminishes.

This is the content of the kinetic theory of rubber created in the thirties by Kuhn, Mark, and Guth. The further development of the physics of macromolecules is connected with the statistical theory of polymeric chains, which allows us to calculate the geometric, electric, and optical properties of polymers—the dimensions, dipole moments, and polarizabilities of macromolecules—on the basis of knowledge of their chemical structure.

The molecular theory of the stretching of rubber is part of general statistical theory developed by a group of Leningrad physicists in the fifties (see [10]). Later, the famous American physicochemist, Nobel laureate Flory, developed the theory further. The monographs of all these scientists, which have been published both in the Soviet Union and in the United States, are a good example of Soviet–American scientific collaboration.

The main idea of this theory is that only some definite turns of the atomic groups around the single bonds are possible, and that rotational isomers or rotamers possess definite conformations that can be established if the chemical structure is known. Thus, in Fig. 15 the rotamers of polyethylene are shown. The group $CH_2\sim$ means the continuation of the chain. It is easy to see that these rotamers are geometrically similar to the rotamers of dibromoethane shown in Fig. 3, and the curve of the potential energy of internal rotation in polyethylene must be similar to the curve shown in Fig. 11.

Thus the macromolecular coil can be treated as a mixture of rotamers. In the calculations of dimensions of the coil or of its dipole moment, the corresponding characteristics of the links of the chain

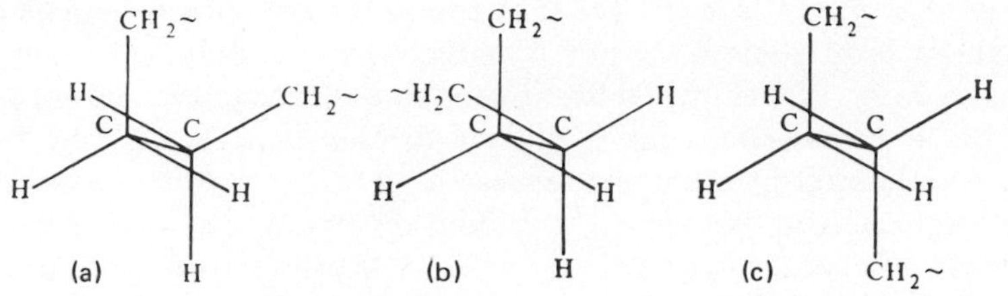

Fig. 15 Rotamers of polyethylene: (a) and (b), *gauche* rotamers; (c), *trans* rotamer.

must be averaged over their possible conformations. Therefore the statistical theory of macromolecules is called the rotational–isomeric theory [10].

The stretching of a rubberlike polymer consists of changing the set of conformations of its links in the rotational isomerization of macromolecules.

The theory takes into account an important property of the macromolecular chain: cooperativity. The turns in the neighboring links are not independent. Some conformations resulting in the close rapprochement of the atoms are impossible. The stretching of rubber—the changes in the conformations of its macromolecules—is also cooperative.

The theory, which we described here in brief, is completely confirmed by experiment. The ideas introduced for the first time in the rotational–isomeric theory of macromolecules proved to be very important for biophysics. The functionality of biopolymers—proteins and nucleic acids—is directly connected with their conformational properties. In this sense the enzymatic catalysis and the high elasticity of rubber have a common origin.

With few exceptions, synthetic polymers form statistical coils in solutions. This does not apply to biopolymers. As we shall see, in the native, that is, the functioning in the cells and organisms, proteins and nucleic acids, the hydrogen bonds and other weak interactions fix some chosen conformations. Statistical coils appear as the result of the denaturation of biopolymers, that is, destruction of their native structure.

If there is a mutual attraction between the links of a polymeric chain due to weak interactions, such as hydrophobic ones, then the coil condenses into the globule. The detailed theory of this coil–globule transition has been developed in the works of Lifshits and his co-workers (see [10]).

These works are rather important for biology. Many proteins

exist in globular form, and the general theory allows us to establish those properties of the protein which are due only to its polymeric structure. The globule differs from the coil; the globule is not a loose but a compact formation similar to the solid body. The protein globule built by the chain representing a text written by the twenty letter alphabet is a kind of aperiodic crystal, to use the expression of Schrödinger. As we shall see further, this is a very important thesis.

CHAPTER 6

Molecular Biophysics and Molecular Biology

Molecular biophysics investigates the structure and physicochemical properties of the molecules of biologically functional substances, such as proteins and nucleic acids, usually by studying substances extracted from cells. There is no difference between studies of the structure and properties of proteins and nucleic acids and studies of any other substances; it is not life itself that is under study but the building blocks of living systems. Elucidation of the peculiarities of these molecules leads directly to the fundamental phenomena of life determined on the molecular level.

The next step is to clarify the physicochemical basis of the biological functions of "biological molecules." The most important biological–biochemical function of proteins is enzyme catalysis; science must explain it. The same concerns other biological functions of the specialized proteins, such as the ability of myoglobin to store oxygen and of hemoglobin to serve as a carrier of oxygen, the immunological function of gamma globulins, and the behavior of the muscle-regulating proteins during muscular contraction.

The question of how nucleic acids function—how they participate in protein biosynthesis—is directly related to biology's fundamental problems: heredity and variability.

Finally, the interactions of various substances in the cells must be studied. This requires physics of the overmolecular cellular structures, that is, an approach to the study of the cell as a whole.

We have already said that proteins are built of a sequence of

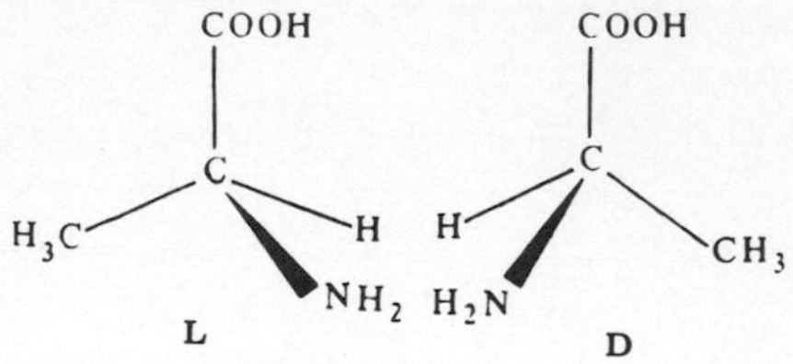

COOH COOH

H_3C C H H C CH_3

NH_2 H_2N

L D

Fig. 16 Spatial configurations of L- and D-alanine.

amino acid residues. Let us emphasize a remarkable feature of amino acids. All amino acids in protein, except glycine, are chiral molecules.* They can exist in two configurations—two forms that cannot coincide as the result of any rotation (in the same way as the right and left hands do not coincide). In Fig. 16, the spatial structure of the left and right amino acid alanine is shown; the R group is CH_3. It is significant that all proteins in nature are built only of left-handed amino acid residues. We shall return to the discussion of this remarkable fact when we consider prebiological evolution in Chapter 11. The right and left molecules differ by the sign of rotation of the plane of polarization of light; the chiral molecules are optically active. Correspondingly, all the proteins (and also the nucleic acids) are optically active, and this feature provides an excellent possibility for studying them.

The protein text, consisting of the sequence of amino acid letters in a chain, is called the primary structure of protein. Now the primary structures of more than 1000 proteins have been deciphered, and they yield extremely valuable information about biological evolution. Similar proteins of various species (for example, the hemoglobins of vertebrates) differ in their primary structures. The nearer the species are to one another, the smaller are the differences. Hence it is possible to restore the family tree of the species according to the primary structures of the homologous proteins. The very term "primary structure" indicates that the proteins also possess higher levels of structure; secondary, tertiary, and even quaternary structures of proteins exist.

The secondary structure is the spatial organization of the protein chain or some part of it. As first shown by Pauling and Corey, there are several fundamental types of secondary structure. In Fig. 17, the so-called alpha helix is shown. The protein chain is folded as a screw

* The word "chirality" is comparatively new in scientific language. Literally it means "handedness"; the root "chir" comes from the ancient Greek *heir*, meaning hand.

helix because of internal rotations around the single bonds C—C and C—N. There is no transformation into a random coil; the definite helical conformation is maintained by hydrogen bonds between the N—H group of one peptide bond and the C=O group of another. In the helix, the hydrogen bonds (broken lines in Fig. 17) connect the first peptide group with the fourth, the second group with the fifth, etc. The hydrogen bonds are directed along the axis of the helix. The existence of this and other secondary structures has been confirmed by theoretical calculations and by direct physical experiments, primarily by x-ray diffraction.

We see that in the alpha helix, the hydrogen bonds fix the definite conformations of the links. The alpha helix in proteins is similar to the aperiodic linear crystal.

Another frequent conformation of proteins is the beta form. Neighboring chains are located in transconformations, forming

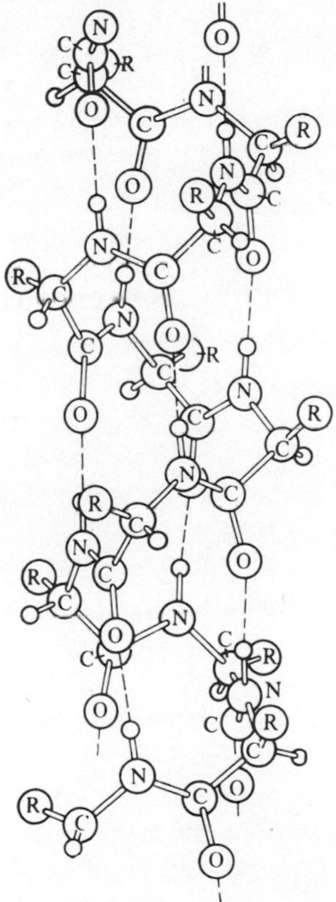

Fig. 17 The alpha helix.

nearly flat structures. The chains are connected by hydrogen bonds, which are directed in this case perpendicular to the *trans* chain. In a single protein molecule, the hairpin-shaped "cross beta forms," are frequently formed.

When a protein is heated or when its surroundings change (for example, by the action of acids, alcalis, urea, etc.), the secondary structure, in particular the alpha helix, is destroyed. The "helix–coil" transition occurs. The physics of these transformations is remarkable—the transition does not occur gradually but according to an "all or nothing" principle. In other words, till some definite temperature (usually lower than 100°C) the helix is stable, and then it destroys as a whole. Why does this occur?

We meet here with a cooperative phenomenon similar to the phase transition. The melting of a crystal and the boiling of a liquid also occur suddenly, in an "all or nothing" way. The physical theory of these phenomena shows that they are due to cooperative interactions of the particles in a system. Thus, for instance, the crystal melts if the free energies of crystal and liquid are equal:

$$H_{\mathrm{crys}} - T_{\mathrm{melt}} S_{\mathrm{crys}} = H_{\mathrm{liq}} - T_{\mathrm{melt}} S_{\mathrm{liq}} \tag{47}$$

where H is enthalpy, T temperature, and S entropy; "crys" stands for crystal, "melt" for melting, and "liq" for liquid. In other words, the crystal melts if the expenditure of energy (enthalpy) is compensated by the gain of entropy

$$H_{\mathrm{liq}} - H_{\mathrm{crys}} = T_{\mathrm{melt}} (S_{\mathrm{liq}} - S_{\mathrm{crys}}) \tag{48}$$

The temperature of melting is

$$T_{\mathrm{melt}} = \frac{H_{\mathrm{liq}} - H_{\mathrm{crys}}}{S_{\mathrm{liq}} - S_{\mathrm{crys}}} \tag{49}$$

When a crystal is heated, the energy (enthalpy) of its atoms increases. The entropy should increase as well because an atom liberated from the crystal lattice possesses more degrees of freedom than an atom bound to the lattice. However, it is impossible to liberate one atom without touching its neighbors; therefore, the entropy does not increase. Since the increased energy is not compensated by increasing entropy, the whole lattice is destroyed only in a cooperative way. Similarly, it is impossible to liberate one link in an alpha helix without breaking the neighboring hydrogen bonds. For such a liberation, energy must be spent to break the hydrogen bonds that fix the given link, but there will be no gain of entropy because the link will not obtain freedom of motion; it is "squeezed" between the neighbor fixed links. The "melting" of an alpha helix can be performed only by the simultaneous break of a series of hydrogen bonds; it is a cooperative process. In the same way, the melting of a kind of bidimensional crystal of the beta form occurs.

The protein chain consists of links whose structures and properties differ; it does not have a single uniform secondary structure throughout. Uniform structure is characteristic only of individual pieces of the chain. Because of the weak interactions between the links, which are not connected by covalent bonds, the protein chain is folded into a compact spatial structure called a globule. This is the tertiary structure. In Fig. 18, the structure of the myoglobin globule, discovered with the help of x-ray diffraction, is shown. By this method, the tertiary structures of about 100 proteins have been studied. In Fig. 18 the alpha-helical parts are denoted by Latin letters. These parts contain about 75% of all amino acid links; the remaining 25% of links belong to the bends and other less ordered parts of the globule.

Myoglobin is used by organisms to store molecular oxygen, O_2 (therefore, myoglobin is contained in great quantities in the bodies of

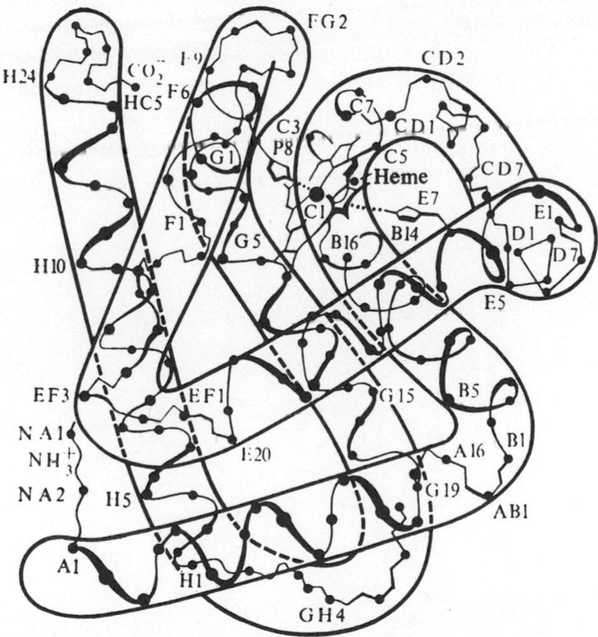

Fig. 18 Structure of the myoglobin molecule. Letters denote helical parts; numbers, the number of each residue in the helix.

whales). Oxygen is bound in myoglobin by the nonproteinic heme group, which is connected to protein. The structure of heme is shown in Fig. 19. Heme contains the so-called porphyrine ring, formed by a series of conjugated π-bonds. Porphyrine compounds absorb light in the visual region; they are colored (see Chapter 2). The red color of raw beefsteak is due to heme in the animal's myoglobin. At the center of the porphyrine ring of heme is the iron atom that binds molecular oxygen.

The porphyrine compounds play various very important roles in life processes. The heme group is also contained, for example, in the blood's hemoglobin and in the respiratory enzymes (cytochromes etc.). Chlorophyll, which is responsible for the green color of photosynthesizing plants, contains a porphyrine ring with a magnesium atom in the center. Vitamin B_{12} contains a porphyrine ring with an atom of cobalt, the blood of *Arthropoda* contains the porphyrine compound of copper, and the blood of *Ascidiae* contains the halves of the porphyrine rings (the dipyrrole group) that bind the vanadium atom.

The physics of the protein globule is very important. It is necessary to understand what a globule is, what forces stabilize its structure, and how this structure is correlated with the primary structure of the chain. The main question is How are the functional properties of the protein, especially its enzymatic properties, determined by the globular structure?

The globule is stabilized mainly by a series of weak interactions. In addition, there are a few additional chemical bonds—the disulfide

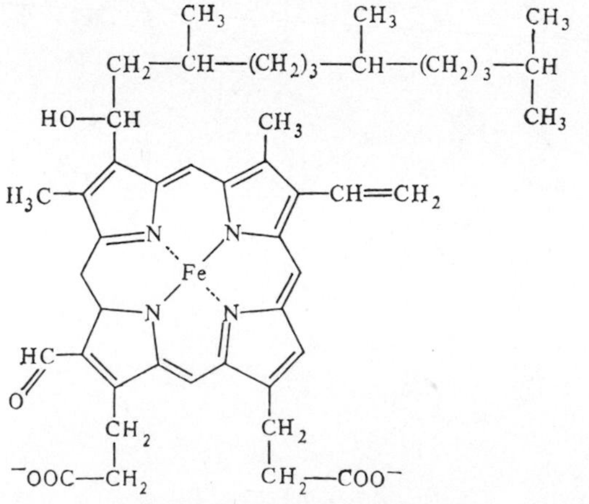

Fig. 19 Structure of heme.

bonds S—S between cysteine residues. Weak interactions are the hydrogen bonds, van der Waals forces, and electrostatic interactions of charged groups. An especially important role is played by hydrophobic interactions.

Proteins function in an aqueous medium. It is impossible to understand their structure without taking into account the influence of water. It is characteristic of contemporary physics to take into consideration the interaction of the studied object with its surroundings—right up to the device used for investigation. Water, as mentioned previously, is a liquid with peculiar properties caused by the presence of a network of hydrogen bonds. We have seen that there are hydrophobic substances not soluble in water, and hydrophilic ones, which "like" water.

Among the twenty amino acid residues, there are also hydrophobic and hydrophilic ones. The first are mainly those residues whose R groups are hydrocarbons. The degree of hydrophobicity, that is, of "hostility" toward water, has been established for all amino acids. Its measure is the difference of the free energies of solutions of amino acid in ethyl alcohol and in water. These values are listed in Table I. Hydrophobicity diminishes from tryptophan to glutamine. The first ten amino acids can be considered hydrophobic, the second ten hydrophilic

Because of the hydrophobic interactions, the flexible protein chain is folded in a globule in such a way that the hydrophobic residues become located mainly in the central part of the globule and do not come in contact with water. This concerns, for instance, myoglobin.

TABLE I

HYDROPHOBICITIES OF AMINO ACIDS[a]

1.	Tryptophan (Trp)	3000	11.	Alanine (Ala)	730
2.	Isoleucine (Ile)	2970	12.	Arginine (Arg)	730
3.	Tyrosine (Tyr)	2870	13.	Cysteine (Cys)	650
4.	Phenylalanine (Phe)	2650	14.	Glutamic acid (Glu)	550
5.	Proline (Pro)	2600	15.	Aspartic acid (Asp)	540
6.	Leucine (Leu)	2420	16.	Threonine (Thr)	440
7.	Valine (Val)	1690	17.	Serine (Ser)	40
8.	Lysine (Lys)	1500	18.	Glycine (Gly)	0
9.	Histidine (His)	1400	19.	Asparagine (Asn)	−10
10.	Methionine (Met)	1300	20.	Glutamine (Gln)	−100

[a] ΔG is in calories per mole.

The heating of the protein solution and the action of acids, alkalis, etc., destroy the globular structure, but the primary structure can remain intact. The denaturation of the protein occurs in the globule–coil transition, which is similar to a phase transition.

Denatured protein is deprived of the biological function of native protein; it is impossible to get a chicken from a boiled egg. However, if the denaturation is performed with great care, the reverse process of renaturation (recovery of the globular structure) is sometimes possible. This shows that there is a correlation between the primary structure of the chain and the spatial structure of the globule. The theory which will predict the structure of globule on the basis of the known primary structure is being developed now with some success. It is much easier to establish the primary structure than the tertiary one. As mentioned above, the primary structures of about 1000 proteins are known, and the spatial structures of about 100.

Let us consider now the most important function of protein—enzymatic activity. The enzyme is a kind of a "black box." There are two ways to examine this box—to supply it with different input signals and study the output signals, or to look inside the box. In our case, both ways are used: the first in studies of enzymatic reactions under different conditions, the second with the help of structural physical methods such as optical, spectroscopical, and x-ray analysis.

The molecules of substrate on which the enzyme is acting enter the cavity that exists in the globule and become bound by its active site—the group of amino acid residues that are distant from one another in the chain but are neighboring in the globule. Substrate binding is a dynamic process. Notwithstanding its compact structure, a globule maintains some conformational flexibility—the links turn around the single bonds at the active site. As a result, the structure of the globule that has absorbed the substrate is changed in such a way that the optimal interaction is provided. The enzyme–substrate complex is formed with the induced fit of mutual structures, and the transformation of substrate into product occurs. Then the product leaves the active site, the enzyme.

The chemical events occurring at the active sites of many enzymes are well studied now. The process at an active site always occurs in a series of stages; the conformation of the protein changes at every stage. The physical theory of enzymatic catalysis is not developed yet, but a series of important results have been obtained. The enzymatic process ultimately means a chemical reaction, that is, the restructuring of the electronic shell of the substrate molecule.

The enzyme provides an effective decrease of the energy of activation. This is achieved as the result of conformational motions in the protein molecule, that is, of the rotation of atomic groups around the single bonds. Therefore, one of the main tasks of molecular biophysics is theoretical and experimental investigation of the electronic-conformational interactions (ECI), which interconnect the corresponding degrees of freedom. In spite of the successes of science in this field, we cannot yet calculate theoretically the rates of the enzymatic reactions, that is, we cannot define quantitatively the decrease of activation energy produced by an enzyme.

The theory of ECI is built on the basis of quantum mechanics and quantum chemistry. In any chemical reaction, displacements of electrons and of atomic nuclei occur. In the proteins, such as enzymes, the shifts of nuclei are specific because the energy necessary for turning around the single bond is markedly smaller than the energy necessary for stretching the bond or for changing the bond angle. Hence the nuclear motions in proteins reduce to conformational motions. The change of the level of electronic energy is followed by conformational changes and vice versa. It can be said that the ECI provides enzymatic catalysis.

The nature of ECI can be explained with the help of a visual model suggested in the works of Gray and Gonda [11]. Let us imagine an electron in a potential box (compare Chapter 2). The standing wave, which is a model for the electron, produces the pressure at the wall of the box [compare formula (7)]

$$
\begin{aligned}
f &= -\frac{dE_n}{dL} \\
&= \frac{n^2h^2}{4mL^3}
\end{aligned}
\tag{50}
$$

The walls of the box in a given state are immobile because the pressure is balanced by external forces. If the electron is excited, its quantum number increases from n to $n' = n + \Delta n$, and the pressure increases, too. Equilibrium is destroyed, the walls shift, and the electronic force does mechanical work. The wall becomes equilibrated again in a new position $L' = L + \Delta L$. The corresponding work is

$$
\begin{aligned}
W &= (f' - f)(L' - L) \\
&= \frac{h^2}{4m}\left(\frac{n'^2}{L'^3} - \frac{n^2}{L^3}\right)\Delta L
\end{aligned}
\tag{51}
$$

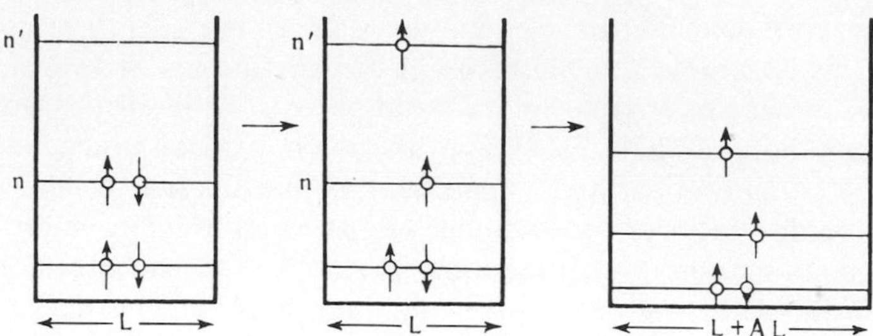

Fig. 20 Scheme ECI.

This process is shown schematically in Fig. 20. The shift of the wall is followed by the decrease of electronic energy, which is inversely proportional to the square of the width L of the box. The wall represents the heavy atomic nuclei. Their displacements in a biopolymer reduce to a change of conformation. Thus the change of the electron state of the system changes its conformational state; the electron energy becomes partly transformed into the conformational one. Simultaneously, the activation barrier of enzymatic reaction is lowered. This can be seen schematically in Fig. 21. Let us replace the rectangular potential well by the parabolic one corresponding to the electron–harmonic oscillator. The left well in the figure represents the state of the reagents, the right that of the products. They are separated by the potential barrier, which is higher the steeper the parabola is. The conformational work performed by the excited electron because of ECI makes the slope of the parabola smaller and diminishes the activation barrier. Thus ECI accelerate the reaction catalyzed by an enzyme. In comparison with a similar reaction proceeding without the participation of an enzyme, the enzymatic reaction is 10^5 and more times faster [10, 12].

Many enzymes contain at their active sites cofactors—atoms and atomic groups of nonproteinic nature. The ions of metals in particu-

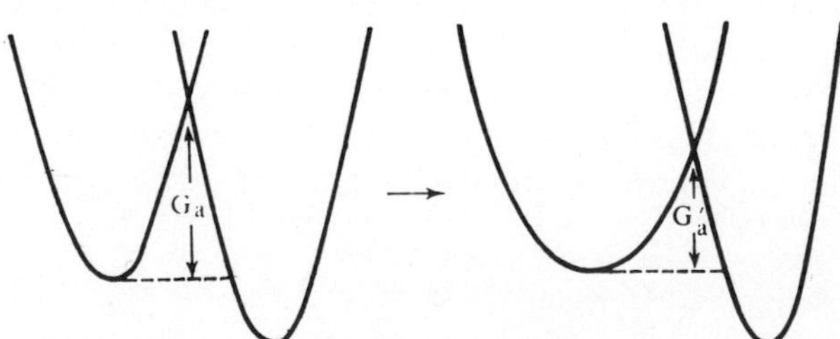

Fig. 21 The lowering of the activation energy because of ECI.

lar can serve as cofactors. Some rather rare elements occur in these cases. For example, in nitrogenase—a very important enzyme—molybdenum acts as cofactor. Nitrogenase catalyzes the fixation of atmospheric nitrogen in the *Rhizobium* bacteria that coexist with the *Leguminosae* plants (beans, clover, etc.). Fixation of nitrogen is one of the bases of life on Earth because nitrogen is necessary for proteins, nucleic acids, etc. Without molybdenum, the fixation of nitrogen would be impossible.

During the last decade, the development of a new field of science—bioinorganic chemistry—began. The main problems of this field concern the structure and properties of the metal-containing proteins. The central place in contemporary inorganic chemistry is occupied by the chemistry of complex or coordination compounds formed by the transient metals, that is, metals possessing variable valence. The scientific theory of this field is completely applicable to the metal-containing proteins. Just these proteins are of the greatest interest in the studies of ECI because the presence of the transient metal allows us to study ECI with the help of such aids as absorption spectra and electronic paramagnetic resonance spectra, etc.

In connection with these problems, we should discuss the system of knowledge of contemporary chemistry. In the eighteenth and the beginning of the nineteenth centuries, the words "organic chemistry" meant the chemistry of substances of animal and vegetable origin, which, it was assumed, could not be obtained artificially. After the discovery of Wöhler, the situation changed, and gradually organic chemistry was transformed into the chemistry of the carbon-containing substances, or more exactly of hydrocarbons and their derivatives. Such substances as CO_2 or $CaCO_3$ belong more naturally to inorganic chemistry. As the result of achievements in biochemistry and molecular biology in the second half of our century, bioorganic chemistry, the organic chemistry of natural compounds, developed. Organic chemistry came to life phenomena again, but on a new basis. In the last decade, bioinorganic joined bioorganic chemistry.

As we have already mentioned, enzymes catalyze all biochemical reactions. Enzymes are excellent catalysts, they work in aqueous medium in soft conditions, and they are very highly selective, acting on one substrate but not on substances with a slightly different structure. Small differences in the molecular structure that can be of no importance in ordinary chemistry happen to be crucial in biochemistry. For instance, C_2H_5OH causes intoxication, and CH_3OH blindness. The chemical properties of these two alcohols are very similar, but in a living system the chemical processes possess a high degree of individualization.

Among the enzymes, there are some that provide feedback in biochemical reactions. These enzymes are called allosteric. Let us consider a chain of biochemical transformations

$$A \rightarrow B \rightarrow C \rightarrow D \rightarrow E \rightarrow F$$

Every transformation is catalyzed by its own enzyme. The systems of reactions exist where the final product F inhibits the action of enzyme catalyzing the first reaction $A \rightarrow B$ of the sequence. In such a way the feedback is realized. If the product F has been formed in excess, the complete process stops at the beginning of the first stage of the sequence.

It has been found that allosteric enzymes possess quaternary structure. This means that their molecules are formed by several globules, each of which possesses its own active site. The globules interact, and the behavior of a given active site depends on the state of other active sites, that is, on the sites' occupation by ligands (substrates, etc.). In this sense, the protein with a quaternary structure possesses cooperative properties. Such a protein is hemoglobin.

Hemoglobin is not an enzyme; it serves as a carrier of molecular oxygen (O_2). The molecule of hemoglobin consists of four globules, each of them similar to the myoglobin globule (see Fig. 18). In every one of the four globules, there is an active site for O_2 binding—the heme group. Hence the hemoglobin molecule can bind four molecules of oxygen. The binding of O_2 occurs in a cooperative way; the affinity of a given active site toward oxygen increases with the binding of O_2 by other active sites. Correspondingly, the curve of saturation of hemoglobin by oxygen possesses an inflection; the saturation curve for myoglobin is smooth (Fig. 22). These properties of hemoglobin are very important in the physiology of respiration.

More detailed information concerning molecular biophysics, and particularly the biophysics of enzymes, can be found in a series of books [10, 13, 14].

Along with the globular proteins, many important functions are executed by the fibrillar proteins, such as the proteins of wool and skin (keratin), the proteins of connective tissue (collagen), and the contractile proteins of muscles (see Chapter 8).

How does the cell produce its proteins? How does it ensure its own existence?

The biosynthesis of proteins occurs with the indispensable participation of the deoxyribonucleic acid (DNA) molecules and of sev-

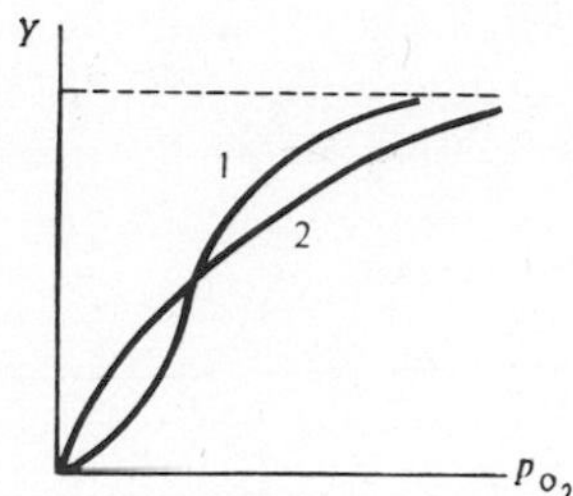

Fig. 22 Curves of saturation by oxygen for hemoglobin (1) and myoglobin (2).

eral types of ribonucleic acids (RNA) that are similar to DNA. Deoxyribonucleic acid is the substance of genes, so we must first understand the function of genes. At the level of organisms, genes are the carriers of heredity—but what is inherited? Such characteristics as the color of eyes or hair are determined by the common action of many genes; but what does a single gene do?

Cells and organisms are chemical machines whose properties are programmed at the molecular level, and every biochemical reaction requires the participation of a definite enzyme; hence the molecular fundamentals of heredity reduce to the synthesis of definite proteins. The genetic program of development is the program of biosynthesis of proteins, and the gene is the carrier of the program of synthesis of a definite protein chain. The discovery of this fundamental thesis is among the most important achievements of biology.

The substance of genes—DNA—is the main component of the chromosomes of eucaryotes, the nuclei-containing cells. The chromosomes consist of DNA and proteins. In procaryotes—the cells without nuclei (bacteria, some algae)—the role of chromosome is performed by pure DNA. What is the structure of DNA?

Like proteins, DNA is a biopolymer. The molecules of DNA are the biggest known by science; their molecular weights can reach 10^9 amu. In contrast to protein, the DNA chain is formed by alternating groups of sugar (deoxyribose) and of phosphate. However, the chain is not monotonous because every sugar contains a nitrogen base as a side group. There are four such bases: adenine (A), guanine (G), thymine (T), and cytosine (C). We do not cite their formulas; they are contained in many books (e.g., [10]). The scheme of the structure of DNA chain is

```
       A     G     G     C     T     T     A
       |     |     |     |     |     |     |
· · · —S—P—S—P—S—P—S—P—S—P—S—P—S— · · ·
```

where S is sugar, P phosphate. Thus the DNA chain, like protein, is also a "text," but written by a four-letter alphabet instead of a twenty-letter one. The primary structure of DNA is the sequence of nitrogen bases or the sequence of nucleotides, the links

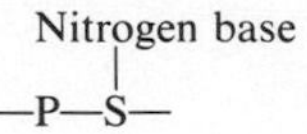

The gene is part of the DNA chain. How does a gene work? How does it provide the biosynthesis of proteins? What determines the high stability of genes, which remain constant through many generations? How does the reduplication of genes during cell division occur?

The answers to all these questions are given by molecular biology and molecular biophysics and are based on knowledge of the secondary structure of DNA obtained with the help of x-ray diffraction. It was found that DNA has the structure of a double helix, in which two chains of DNA are coiled together like a double electric wire. Before this investigation, it was known that in DNA the content of A is equal to the percentage of T and the content of G is equal to that of C (Chargaff's rule). It has been found that the two chains of the helix are complementary; the G of one chain is always located opposite the C of another; the same holds for the bases A and T. The pairs A–T and G–C are connected by hydrogen bonds. The scheme of the double helix is shown in Fig. 23. The history of its discovery was beautifully described by Watson [15], who established the double helix structure of DNA together with Crick and Wilkins.

The discovery of the double helix structure of DNA was not important only for understanding its structure. This structure is very peculiar, and its understanding led immediately to very important qualitative conclusions concerning the properties of DNA. The existence of a double helix secured by hydrogen bonds (in contrast to the alpha helix of proteins, the hydrogen bonds in DNA are directed not along the helix but perpendicular to it) explains the stability of DNA and of genes. Thus the answer to Schrödinger's question (Chapter 1) has been obtained, and the model of DNA replication—its doubling at every cell division—can immediately be built. This model is shown in Fig. 24.

We assume that the changes of conditions of the medium lead to the break of the hydrogen bonds that fix the double helix. The helix unwinds into two chains (Fig. 24a). The nucleotides of every chain

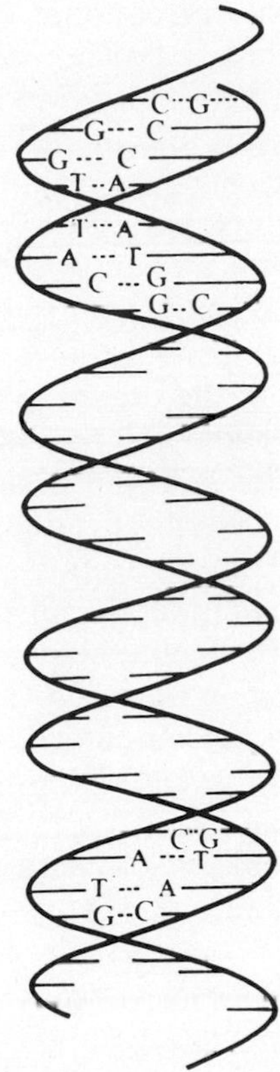

Fig. 23 Double helix of DNA.

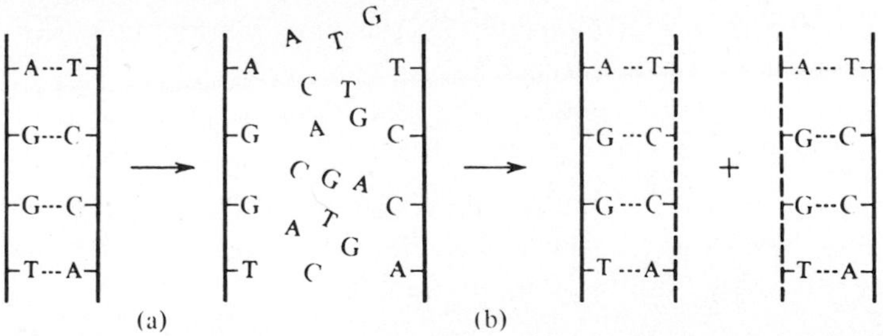

Fig. 24 DNA replication: (a) separation of the chains, and (b) formation of new double helices.

bind the monomers from the surrounding solution in such a way that G binds C and A binds T, and vice versa (Fig. 24b). Then the polycondensation of monomers occurs, and two new double helices, identical with the initial ones, are formed. This model has been totally confirmed by experiment. Thus, the physical investigation that uncovered the double helix structure of DNA happened to be connected with the fundamental problems of biology.

The stability of genes is not absolute. In the genes there appear mutations—changes of the structure of the gene and, hence, of the hereditary characteristics of the organism. Mutations are produced by chemical or radiation action, and they also appear spontaneously as a result of thermal motion. These last mutations are created as a result of mistakes during DNA replication. For instance, if G accidentally binds T and not C, this alteration of the secondary structure becomes fixed in the following replications.

Like the alpha helix, the double helix of DNA can "melt": during the heating of the solution up to 65–70°C, a sharp cooperative helix–coil transition occurs, accompanied by decrease of the viscosity of solution, alteration of its optical properties, etc.

Along with the formulation and investigation of the fundamental problems in molecular biophysics, a series of physical methods of studies of biopolymers and the theory of these methods were worked out. These methods reduce mainly to the interactions of the molecules of proteins and nucleic acids with light of various wavelengths, from x rays and gamma-radiation to radio waves. We shall limit ourselves to enumerating these methods and summarizing their characteristics.

X-ray analysis is a difficult method, limited by the possibilities of obtaining monocrystals of proteins and nucleic acids. At the same time, this method gives especially detailed and valuable information about the structure of molecules. Nowadays works are performed that apply the so-called synchrotron x-ray radiation, which allows the study of rapid structural changes of biopolymers and of the systems built by them (e.g., muscle).

Electron microscopy allows us to obtain photos not only of the single molecules of proteins and nucleic acids, but also of the heavy atoms introduced into biopolymers as labels.

Electronic and vibrational spectroscopy are the studies of ultraviolet and infrared absorption spectra of biopolymers, and also of their Raman spectra obtained with laser sources of radiation.

Luminescence spectra of biopolymers (proteins) themselves, and of biopolymers with introduced fluorescent labels, also belong to electronic spectra.

The investigations of *natural optical activity* and of *circular dichroism* of biopolymers are widely used. These phenomena are determined by the chirality of biological molecules.

Magnetic spectropolarimetry, that is, investigations of *the magnetic optical activity* (*Faraday effect*) and of *magnetic circular dichroism,* are methods especially effective in the studies of the heme-containing proteins (such as hemoglobin, myoglobin, and cytochromes).

Spectroscopy of nuclear paramagnetic resonance provides valuable information about biopolymers and their interactions.

Spectroscopy of electron paramagnetic resonance deals mainly with polymers that have "spin labels," that is, stable free radicals.

Gamma resonance spectroscopy (*Mössbauer effect*) is especially suitable for iron-containing proteins.

This list is not exhaustive. It is very important for molecular biophysics and molecular biology that the physical methods enable us to study not only the static structures of biopolymers but also the dynamics of their conformational transformations.

These methods have been described in detail in other works [10].

CHAPTER 7

Biosynthesis of Proteins and the Genetic Code

As discussed in Chapter 6, DNA contains the program of protein biosynthesis. Both DNA and proteins are informational macromolecules, but their texts are written in different languages—DNA in a four-letter language, and protein in a twenty-letter one. The programming role of DNA means that there must be a correlation between the two texts: the text of DNA becomes translated into protein language. How many letters of the DNA language, that is, how many nucleotides, correspond to one letter of protein language, that is, to one amino acid residue?

One nucleotide is too few to correspond to an amino acid: there are only four different nucleotides but twenty amino acids. Two nucleotides are also too few: the number of combinations of four by two is $4^2 = 16$, which is insufficient for the coding of twenty amino acids. If three nucleotides are responsible for one amino acid, we get a number which is more than sufficient: $4^3 = 64$. We come to the problem of the genetic code, which correlates the nucleotide and amino acid texts. This problem was formulated by physicists (Gamow and others) immediately after the double helix was discovered in 1953.

Many scientists tried to solve the problem of the genetic code theoretically using methods similar to those used in decoding ancient inscriptions or secret codes. (Recall Edgar Allan Poe's *The Gold Bug* and Conan Doyle's *The Dancing Manikins!*) Champollion (whose predecessor was the physicist Young, discoverer of the interference of light), who deciphered the ancient Egyptian hieroglyphic writings, had at his disposal the Rosetta stone, where the same inscription was written in hieroglyphs, in simplified demotic writing, and in ancient Greek. Besides that, Champollion knew the Coptic language, which has much in common with ancient Egyptian. These methods could not be applied in the case of DNA. The elementary way of Sherlock Holmes could not be used because in contrast to human languages there is no correlation of the letters in biopolymers: in the protein chain, any amino acid can follow the given one, and the same is true for the nucleotides in DNA. It was not possible to go the way of Champollion because there was no Rosetta stone and no language similar to the language of DNA. The primary structures of the DNA and RNA samples were established and the texts read only after the code was deciphered.

The contribution of physics to the problem of the genetic code consisted not of solving the problem but of formulating it. The solution was obtained not by physical but by biological and chemical methods.

First the molecular mechanism of the protein biosynthesis had to be understood.

This mechanism is not simple. Biosynthesis of protein proceeds in a series of stages, the first of which is transcription. At one of two chains of the double helix of DNA, the complementary chain of the so-called informational or messenger RNA—mRNA—is synthesized. RNA differs from DNA in its sugar groups: RNA contains ribose instead of deoxyribose. In addition, in RNA uracil (U) replaces the thymine (T) of DNA.

Transcription (and also replication of DNA) occurs with the participation of specific enzymes—polymerases—which contain the Zn^{++} ion at the active site. It has been found that transcription proceeds simultaneously with conformational changes of the DNA chain.

In mRNA the same genetic text is written as in DNA, but in RNA the text is contained not in chromosomes but in the cytoplasm. The messenger RNA becomes united with compact intracellular particles called ribosomes. The ribosomes are built by proteins and ribosomal RNA, rRNA, which is also synthesized at the DNA chain. The ribosomes with mRNA form the polysome, a structure similar to a string of beads. The role of string is played by mRNA, the role of beads by ribosomes. The scheme of the polysome structure is shown in Fig. 25.

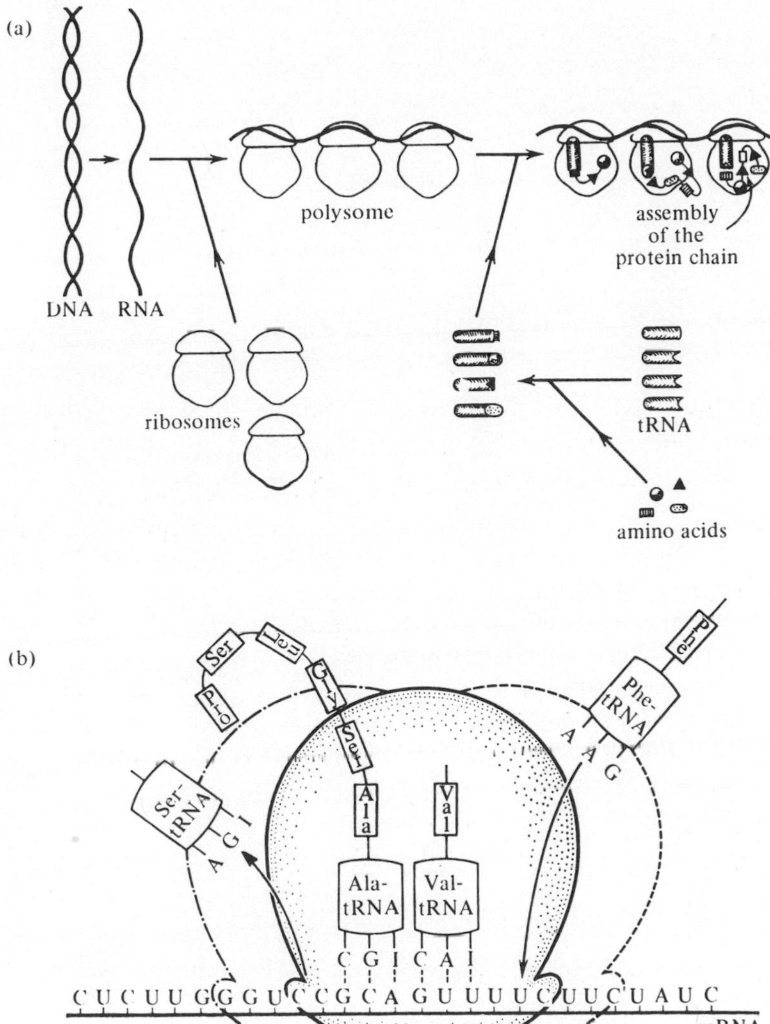

Fig. 25 Protein synthesis: (a) synthesis; (b) the work of a ribosome.

Simple physicochemical reasoning shows that the amino acids themselves cannot be connected in a polypeptide chain. Such a connection is polycondensation, a process that releases water. However, protein biosynthesis occurs in an aqueous medium, and the abundance of water will force the reaction to proceed not with the

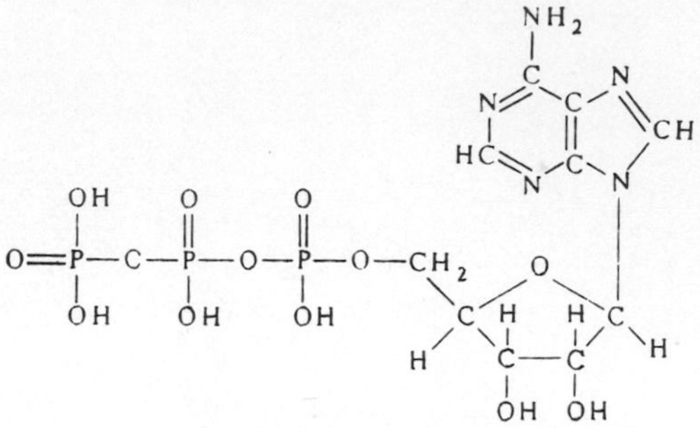

Fig. 26 The structure of ATP.

formation of a peptide bond but in the reverse direction—hydrolysis of the bond:

$$\text{—CO—NH— } + H_2O \rightarrow \text{—COOH} + H_2N\text{—}$$

This means that the free energy is not lessened but increased in the course of polycondensation. Such a reaction is impossible. For the biosynthesis of protein, the deficit of free energy must be compensated. Amino acids obtain surplus free energy through hydrolytical splitting of adenosine triphosphate (ATP).

ATP, whose structural formula is shown in Fig. 26, is a universal biological accumulator of the energy used in various processes. ATP contains three phosphate groups. Free energy of the order of 10 kcal/mole is released during the splitting of the first and second phosphate group from ATP,

$$\text{ATP} + H_2O \rightarrow \text{ADP} + P_i$$

$$\text{ADP} + H_2O \rightarrow \text{AMP} + P_i$$

where ADP is adenosine diphosphate, AMP adenosine monophosphate, and P_i phosphate.

In the cell, the amino acids become activated with the help of specific enzymes, and amino-acyl adenylates are formed.

$$\text{Amino acid} + \text{ATP} + \text{enzyme} \rightarrow \text{amino-acyl adenylate} + \text{enzyme} + PP_i$$

where PP_i is diphosphate. The structure of amino-acyl adenylate is shown in Fig. 27. The same enzymes have a second function: they bind amino-acyl adenylates to the transfer RNA's (tRNA's).

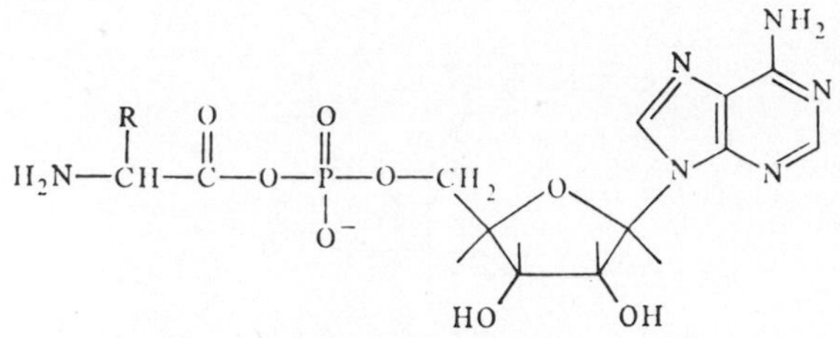

$$H_2N—\underset{R}{CH}—\overset{O}{\overset{\|}{C}}—O—\overset{O}{\overset{\|}{\underset{O^-}{P}}}—O—CH_2 \text{ (ribose, HO, OH; adenine, } NH_2\text{)}$$

Fig. 27 The structure of amino-acyl adenylate.

The following reaction occurs:

$$H_3\overset{+}{N}—CHR—CO—O—\overset{O}{\overset{\|}{\underset{O^-}{P}}}—O—\text{Adenosine} + \text{tRNA}$$

$$\rightarrow H_3\overset{+}{N}—CHR—CO—\text{tRNA} + \text{AMP}$$

The transfer RNA's are the third kind of RNA molecules participating in protein synthesis. One or several tRNA's correspond to every amino acid and bind the suitable amino-acyl adenylate. The transfer RNA's are comparatively small molecules: they contain approximately 80 nucleotides and their molecular weights are of the order 25,000.

These molecules have been studied in detail. They have the form of a clover leaf, as shown in Fig. 28. Part of the nucleotides form the double helix structures, which are the linear sections in Fig. 28 where U is connected by hydrogen bonds with A, and G with C; and I, ψ, G*, U*, and C* are noncanonical, rare, minor nucleotides. The spatial structure of tRNA was established recently with the help of x-ray structural analysis (A. Rich).

An amino acid is bound to the end of the tRNA molecule. The molecules of tRNA bringing amino acids are connected one after another with mRNA by the hydrogen bonds. They become bound to those regions of mRNA that are placed inside the ribosome. The binding occurs through three nucleotides: three sequential nucleotides of mRNA—the codon—are bound with three nucleotides of tRNA—the anticodon—located in the upper petal of the clover leaf. The ribosomes move along the mRNA chain "reading" the genetic text. Simultaneously, two tRNAs with their amino acids are located in one ribosome. Polycondensation of amino acids occurs, and at every ribosome its own protein chain grows. If a polysome contains ten ribosomes, then ten protein chains are synthesized sequentially

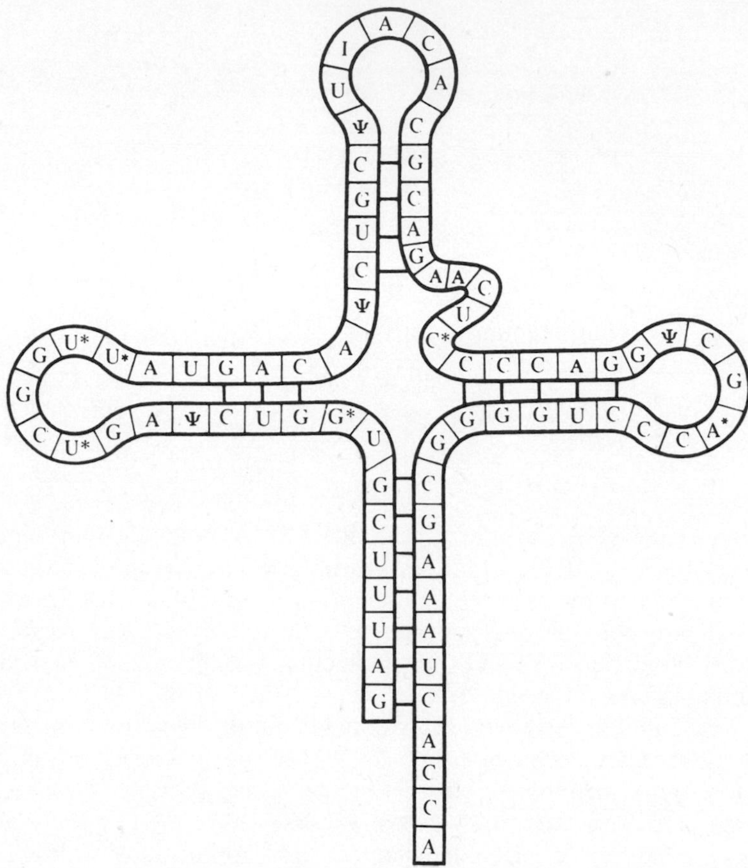

Fig. 28 Clover leaf structure of the valine tRNA.

at it. The nucleic acid text is translated into the proteinic one. The model of protein biosynthesis is shown in Fig. 25.

The discovery of the translation mechanism is one of the greatest achievements of molecular biology. At the basis of this mechanism is the genetic code, the mystery of which was unraveled by deceiving the cell. Nirenberg took a cell-free system containing ribosomes, all types of tRNA, and the necessary enzymes. Instead of mRNA, synthetic polynucleotides were introduced into the system. Various amino acids with radioactive labels were also introduced in sequence. The transfer of the label into the precipitate, that is, the introduction of the given amino acid into the insoluble polypeptide chain under the template action of the given polynucleotide, was determined.

The first experiments with polyuridylic acid (poly U) already showed that only phenylalanine becomes polycondensated under its action. Before that, the study of mutations showed that the code is a triplet code, that is, the given amino acid is coded by three sequential nucleotides of the DNA chain and hence of mRNA. Thus the triplet or codon UUU codes Phe.

Later the coding action of copolymers, which contain various nucleotides, and of short chains with a known sequence of nucleotides were studied. These studies, for which Nirenberg and Khorana won the Nobel prize, allowed them to decipher the genetic code.

The problem of the genetic code was solved in 1965—only twelve years after its formulation.

As we have mentioned, the genetic code is a triplet code; every amino acid is coded by one or several codons. As the number of triplets formed by four nucleotides is $4^3 = 64$, the code is degenerate, that is, a given amino acid can be coded by several codons. Thus Arg, Ser, and Leu are coded by six codons each. Many amino acids are coded by four and two codons, Ile is coded by three, and Met and Trp are coded by one codon each. Three codons, namely UAA, UAG, and UGA, do not code any amino acid, but determine the termination of the growing protein chain.

The genetic code mRNA-protein is presented in Table II, where every codon is represented as *xyz*. Before considering Table II, let us discuss the important features of biologically functional molecules, found in the studies of enzymatic catalysis and of protein biosynthesis.

The common feature of these processes and a host of other biological phenomena is molecular recognition. As we have said, in contrast to the man-made robot, cells and organisms function on the basis of molecular signalization. Hence the corresponding receptive systems and the transformers of molecular signals must recognize these signals and distinguish the molecules. What does the recognition of a molecule mean? It might be said that in the simple reaction

$$NH_3 + HCl \rightarrow NH_4Cl$$

the ammonia molecule recognizes the hydrogen chloride molecule, and the formation of NH_4Cl is the result of this recognition. However, in an ordinary chemical reaction, both the recognizing

TABLE II

GENETIC CODE

x \ *y*	A	C	G	U	*z*
A	**Lys 3.5**	Thr 2.6	Arg 1.9	**Ile 3.4**	A
	Asn 3.9	Thr 2.1	Ser 2.0	**Ile 4.1**	C
	Lys 2.9	Thr 1.7	Arg 2.0	**Met 3.1**	G
	Asn 3.9	Thr 2.1	Ser 2.0	**Ile 4.1**	U
C	**Gln 4.2**	Pro 3.8	Arg 1.8	**Leu 1.8**	A
	His 3.2	Pro 3.3	Arg 1.9	**Leu 1.5**	C
	Gln 4.2	Pro 3.8	Arg 2.5	**Leu 2.1**	G
	His 3.2	Pro 3.3	Arg 1.9	**Leu 1.5**	U
G	Gln 1.4	Ala 1.6	Gly 1.7	**Val 2.2**	A
	Asp 1.6	Ala 1.6	Gly 1.4	**Val 2.3**	C
	Glu 1.4	Ala 1.6	Gly 2.5	**Val 1.9**	G
	Asp 1.6	Ala 1.6	Gly 1.4	**Val 2.3**	U
U	Term	Ser 3.6	Term	**Leu 3.0**	A
	Tyr 4.0	Ser 3.2	Cys 3.2	**Phe 2.8**	C
	Term	Ser 3.9	**Trp 6.6**	**Leu 2.3**	G
	Tyr 4.0	Ser 3.2	Cys 3.2	**Phe 2.3**	U

and the recognized systems cease to exist, whereas molecular recognition is weak, nonchemical interaction in which both systems or the recognizing system is maintained. Recognition occurs at the active site of the enzyme, where different amino acid residues forming this site interact with a substrate. The protein globule is also formed by intramolecular recognition.

We encounter the same phenomena in the structure and properties of nucleic acids. The "Watson–Crick pairs" A–T and G–C arise as the result of molecular recognition; one chain of DNA recognizes the second, complementary chain. The scheme of DNA replication shown in Fig. 24 is based on molecular recognition. In the process of transcription of the DNA text into the text of mRNA, the chain of mRNA is synthesized on the DNA chain as a template on the basis of recognition of the complementary pairs A–U, T–A, G–C, and C–G. Finally, tRNA carrying an amino acid is bound to the mRNA in a ribosome by interaction of the complementary triplet—the anticodon of tRNA—with the mRNA codon.

For the organism as a whole, hormones serve as molecular signals. The reception of smell and taste is molecular reception based on recognition of corresponding molecules.

Further physical and chemical investigation in this area is necessary.

The second feature that determines the main biological processes—especially protein synthesis, that is, heredity and variability—is template synthesis. During DNA replication and during its transcription into the text of mRNA and other kinds of RNA, the DNA chain serves as the template at which, as a result of nucleotide recognition and subsequent polycondensation, the new chain is assembled. The assembly of the new chain proceeds link after link, and the genetic information becomes transcribed from the DNA language into that of RNA. The translation of the mRNA text into the protein text is also based on template synthesis.

Chemistry and physics encounter template synthesis only in the studies of living systems. Template synthesis is determined by the structure and properties of nucleic acids, and ultimately by molecular recognition.

It is evident that the nucleic acids DNA and mRNA play a "legislative role," and the proteins an "executive" one. The transfer of genetic information occurs always from nucleic acids to proteins, but not in the reverse direction:

$$\text{DNA} \rightarrow \text{mRNA} \rightarrow \text{Protein}$$

In a series of oncogenic viruses, the so-called reverse transcription occurs: the initial text is written in RNA, which determines the synthesis of DNA:

$$\text{RNA} \rightarrow \text{DNA} \rightarrow \text{mRNA} \rightarrow \text{Protein}$$

The reverse process, from protein to nucleic acids, never occurs because of the basic difference between the structures of the two types of biopolymers: protein is unable to serve as a template for synthesis.

Let us return to the genetic code, given in Table II. Analysis of the table shows that the codon–amino acid dictionary is not accidental.

Evidently, only the primary structure of the protein is coded genetically. At the same time, natural selection in evolution concerns the biological properties of the protein, determined by its tertiary and quaternary structure. There would be no connection between genetics and evolutionary biology if there were no correlation between the primary and spatial structures of the protein. Such a correlation has been established (see Chapter 6). It is caused by specific weak interactions of the amino acid residues in the chain, particularly by their hydrophobic interactions.

Let us consider the hydrophobicities of amino acids (Chapter 6, Table I). Considering the first ten amino acids (presented by boldface letters) as hydrophobic, we see that their positions in Table II are not accidental. If in the codon *xyz* the second letter, *y*, is U, then the amino acid is hydrophobic with any *x* and *z*.

According to the data quoted above, the difference of hydrophobicities of amino acids is, on the average, 1280 cal/mole. Let us look at the results of mutations, single substitutions of the nucleotides in codons, and the corresponding substitutions of amino acids in the protein chain. If the substitutions occur in position *x*, the average difference of hydrophobicities of the coded amino acids is 1000 cal/mole; substitutions in positions *y* and *z* give 1280 and 340 cal/mole, respectively. On the average, for substitution in all three positions we get 870 cal/mole, which is markedly smaller than the 1280 cal/mole corresponding to accidental replacement. A mutation resulting in a big change of hydrophobicity is evidently more dangerous for the spatial structure of the protein than a mutation with a small change. The genetic code is arranged in such a way that it provides protection against the most dangerous mutations. The genetic code is ultimately determined by specific properties of water, through hydrophobic interactions.

Many books are devoted to molecular biology. Foremost among them is the book by Watson [16].

We shall return to the problem of the genetic code once more in Chapter 12.

CHAPTER 8

Cellular Biophysics and Bioenergetics

Studies performed at the molecular level reveal the physicochemical fundamentals of the most important biological phenomena—heredity, variability, and enzymatic catalysis. We begin by acquiring an understanding of the molecular–biological laws, which we then use to approach a higher level of biological organization—the cell.

Let us consider two very general problems: first, the regulation of gene action, which determines ontogenic development, the differentiation of the cells, morphogenesis, and carcinogenesis; second, the subject of bioenergetics, the storage of the chemical energy in the cell and its use for various kinds of work.

The whole multicellular organism is programmed genetically; the genetic information contained in DNA determines the pattern of development of the organism and its hereditary characteristics. Evidently, this information is already contained in the initial embryonic cell, the zygote, which is the result of the union of the maternal ovicell and the paternal spermatozoon. The organism arises as the result of division of the zygote and subsequent cells, and their differentiation and specialization. During every division of the cell, the genetic material—chromosomes and DNA—is doubled. This means that every specialized cell contains the complete initial set of genes.

However, in a given cell only the proteins responsible for its specialized behavior are synthesized; but the set of genes contained in the zygote and in all other cells serves as the program of synthesis of all proteins in all the organism's cells. Hence, the only genes working in a given cell are those that determine the synthesis of a small fraction of proteins necessary for the cell's functioning; the other genes are suppressed or repressed. The genetic program is regulated.

This reasoning was proved by the experiments on plants made by Stewart and later Butenko. A small piece of the specialized tissue of a carrot root was taken and put in a nutritious medium, which contained coconut milk (the plant's liquid endosperm, which contains growth substances). The tissue of the carrot grew rapidly and increased its mass eightyfold in twenty days. The cells of the tissue divided but did not differentiate. An ugly accumulation of cells of one type arose as in a cancerous tumor.

Then, a single cell was taken from this accumulation and put into a special medium. In this medium the complete carrot plant was grown, with leaves, flowers, and seeds.

These surprising experiments show that gene regulators are present in the cytoplasm of the specialized cell and that the regulatory action is performed by the interaction of the cells. A change of medium results in the "transformation" of the specialized cell in a zygote.

However we shall be less astonished if we remember that strawberries propagate by runners, potatoes from eyes, and begonias by leaves. Of course, the vegetative reproduction of plants raises a series of complicated biochemical and biophysical problems.

There is no vegetative reproduction in the case of higher animals. Gurdon removed the nucleus from the nonfertilized ovicell of a frog and substituted for it a nucleus taken from the specialized cell of a tadpole's intestinal epithelium. The cell divided, and at the end a normal frog was obtained from it. The change of the genes' regulation by cytoplasm resulted in their activation.

It is known now that the regulators of the genes' work are special proteins (also synthesized as the result of transcription of the genetic text). Chromosomes are built by DNA and various proteins. Chromosomes are complicated overmolecular systems containing specific proteins—histones, which are necessary for the maintenance and changes of the chromosome structures, and nonhistone proteins, which seem to have the regulatory role of activating and suppressing the biosynthetic work of genes. Moreover, there are regulatory proteins in the cytoplasm surrounding the chromosomes.

In our time, molecular biology is becoming more and more "biological"—it is turning naturally from the study of single biopolymer molecules to the study of biological processes determined by interactions of biopolymers and of the overmolecular structures built by them. Now molecular biology studies the molecular fundamentals of cell differentiation, of ontogenesis as a whole. Work in this field is just beginning. What role does physics play in this work?

We meet here again with the problem of recognition, this time recognition between DNA and the histones and regulatory proteins. Up to now there has not been sufficient information about the primary and spatial structures of both kinds of biopolymers; investigations of this recognition are just beginning. The structure of DNA is well known, but the molecular structure of chromosomes is not yet clearly established.

An important physical problem that is solved now only with the help of theoretical models is elucidation of the general features of molecular regulation resulting in specialized protein synthesis. It is connected with the mathematical models of ontogenesis, cell differentiation, morphogenesis, and carcinogenesis.

We must emphasize that the formulation of clear physical problems in this field has up to now been frequently hindered by the insufficiency of biological knowledge.

Let us turn now to bioenergetics. The treatment of this field must begin with studies of the cellular membranes because the storage of chemical energy and the performance of definite types of work is localized in the special cellular membranes.

Every cell possesses a definite individuality because it is separated from the surrounding world by a membrane cover. The cellular membrane is a complicated, organized structure composed of fatty substances (lipids) and proteins.

Biological membranes are built by two layers of lipids and proteins interacting with lipids. Lipids are molecules that possess polar groups at one end (the head), and hydrophobic hydrocarbon tails at the other. The tails are directed inside the membrane, the heads outside (Fig. 29). The thickness of the membrane is of the order of 100 Å.

Physical studies have shown that the membrane exists in a liquid–crystalline state. At physiological temperatures, the lipids of many kinds of membranes are melted and the viscosity of a membrane is of the same order as the viscosity of vegetable oil. It can be said that proteins "swim in a lipid sea."

The active properties of the membrane are due to proteins and their interactions with lipids. A membrane is not a passive cover. It

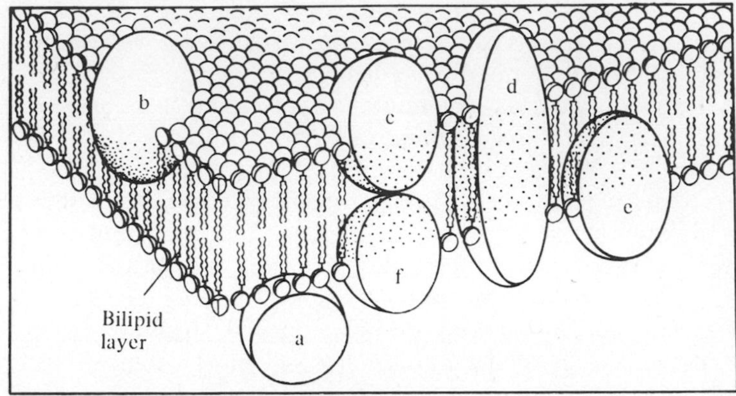

Fig. 29 Structure of a biological membrane; a, b, . . . , f are protein molecules.

is permeable to the ions of metals (primarily Na^+, K^+, Mg^{2+}, and Ca^{2+}) and to other substances. The exchange of cellular substances with the external world occurs through the membrane, which is responsible for active transport, whereby a series of ions and molecules are actively sucked into the cell or thrown out of it. The direction of active transport is not from higher to lower concentration of the solution, but the reverse. Active transport is like a pump; a source of energy is necessary for the pump to work. It is known that active transport, like other types of work in the cell, use the energy liberated during ATP splitting (Chapter 7). The splitting of ATP occurs with the necessary participation of the enzyme ATPase, one of the proteins contained in membranes. It was discovered that the liberated energy is used in active transport, but the complete molecular mechanism of the process has not yet been settled. The ions of the alkaline and alkaline-earth metals move along special channels in the membranes.

Because of active transport, the concentration of the K^+ ion inside the cell is much higher than in the surrounding medium, and the concentration of the Na^+ ions is much lower. Let us consider the data (see Table III) concerning the frog's muscle and the squid's axon (an axon is a long appendix of a nerve cell). As a result, a potential difference appears at the membrane of the cell; the ions are charged and therefore the charges are different at the internal and external surfaces of the membrane. The internal surface becomes charged negatively, the external surface positively. Thus electric work is performed on account of the ATP energy.

TABLE III

ION CONCENTRATIONS[a]

	Na^+	K^+	Cl^-
	Frog's muscle		
Inside	9.2	140	3–4
Outside	120	2.5	120
	Squid's axon		
Inside	50	400	40–100
Outside	460	10	540

[a] In mmole/l.

Biopotentials are tremendously important to medicine: electrocardiography and electroencephalography are based on their measurement. The propagation of the nervous impulse is due to changes of the biopotentials.

The nervous impulse is an electrical, or more exactly, an electrochemical phenomenon. It is propagated by the axons with a velocity of the order of 20 m/s in mammals. One might imagine that the nerve is a conductor of the second kind (an electrolyte), a pipe containing an electrolyte—but it is not. The resistance of the liquid inside the axon is approximately 10^8 times higher than that of a copper wire of the same cross section. The axon membrane is a bad insulator: the leakage of current from the axon can be 10^6 greater than from the cover of a good wire. Nevertheless, the nervous impulse is transmitted in the big animals a distance of several meters without damping and distortion. This has been shown by direct electrophysiological experiments.

The propagation of the impulse begins in the axon's membrane, which can be excited electrically by an electric potential. If the excitation potential is higher than some threshold value, that is, if the potential at the membrane changes from -80 to $+50$ mV (as in the squid's axon), then the cell becomes excited, the permeabilities of the potassium and sodium channels change, and the axon generates its own impulse, which enhances the initial external impulse. The action potential appears to be $+40$ mV. This potential is propagated along the axon with constant velocity.

The appearance of the impulse is connected with the depolarization of the membrane as it recharges at the site of excitation. The K^+ ions leave the cell, and the Na^+ ions enter it. As a result, the internal surface of the membrane becomes positively charged, and the external surface negatively. The impulse excites the neighbor section of the axon, changing the membrane's permeability. After several milliseconds, directly behind the moving impulse the directions of the flows of K^+ and Na^+ change, and the membrane returns to its initial polarized state. The motion of the impulse along the axon is similar to the motion of flame along Bikford's cord. The scheme of this process is shown in Fig. 30. The mechanism of the generation and propagation of the impulse was investigated by many scientists, including Hodgkin, Huxley, and Tasaki [17–19].

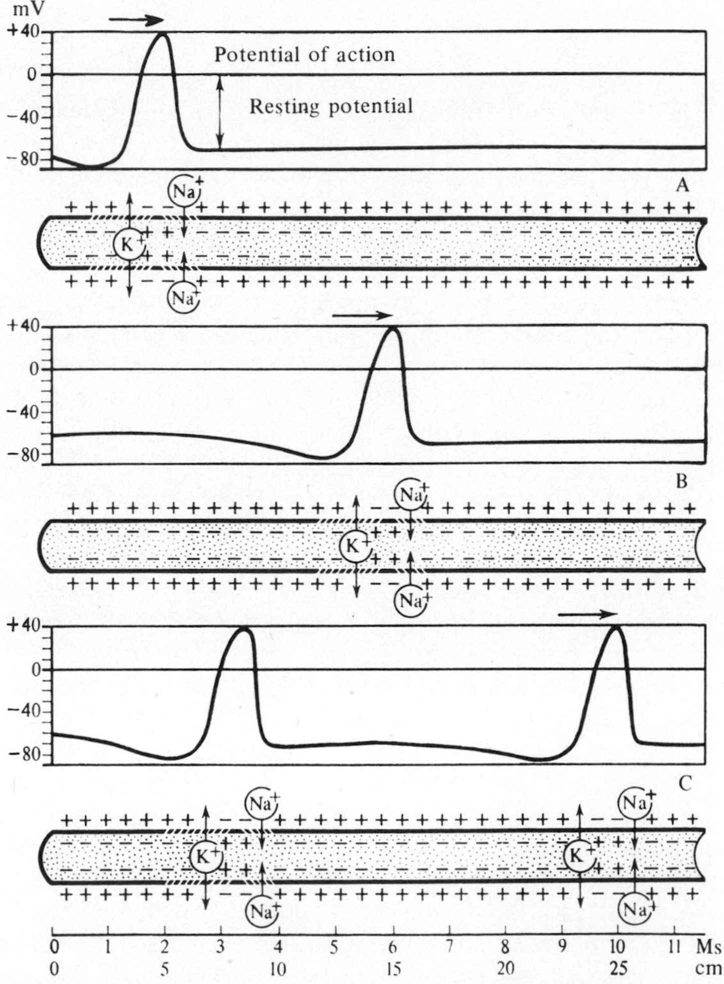

Fig. 30 Propagation of the nervous impulse: A, B, C, are membrane potentials.

Many physical problems are connected with the generation and propagation of the nervous impulse, beginning with the molecular mechanisms of the changes of ionic permeability of the membrane and ending with the theory of complicated nervous networks. A model theory of the active transport of the alkaline cations that explains a series of experimental facts, has been suggested. However, we do not yet possess a molecular physics of membranes that takes into account their liquid–crystalline structure. In addition, much work remains to be done studying the generation of nervous impulse. In contrast, the propagation of nervous impulse is now well studied, and physical theory allows us to calculate the velocity of propagation in accordance with experiment if the electrical characteristics of the axon's membrane are known [19].

Membrane physics and the physics of the nervous impulse connected with it are broad and important fields of contemporary science.

Now we turn our attention to the restoration of ATP, the accumulator of chemical energy in the living cell. Were the supply of ATP in the cells not continuously restored, life on earth could not exist.

The reverse of ATP splitting (described in Chapter 7)—ADP phosphorylation—occurs in two very important processes: respiration in animals and plants and photosynthesis in green plants. Both these processes are localized in the membranes of subcellular organelles. Respiration brings O_2 into the organism. In the mitochondria membranes, organic substances are oxidized to H_2O and CO_2. Simultaneously, oxidative phosphorylation—the transformation of ADP into ATP—occurs. The complicated biochemistry of these processes is almost completely decoded. As physics sees it, the chain of transformations of organic substances, in which a series of oxidative–reductive enzymes (cytochrome *c*, etc.) participate, is an electron transfer chain known as the respiration chain. At the final link of the chain, the electrons reduce oxygen and water is formed. In the respiration chain the electrochemical potential drops, and the balance of energy shows that the ATP accumulator becomes charged on account of this fall.

The description of these complicated processes can be found in the excellent biology treatise written by Villee and Dethier [20]. Biophysics of cells and of more complicated systems is treated in monographs [14, 19].

Beginning with Engelhardt's work (1931), in which the coupling of phosphorylation and respiration was shown for the first time, and ending with contemporary physical studies of the respiratory chain, the processes proceeding in the membranes of mitochondria remain one of the central problems of biophysics and bioenergetics. Science is still far from a complete understanding of these processes. The complexity of the problems is due to their nonequilibrium, dynamic character, which makes molecular interpretation both of oxidative phosphorylation and of photosynthesis difficult. There are grounds for thinking that the electrons move in these systems by quantum-mechanical tunneling (subbarrier penetration of electronic waves). The height and width of the barrier decrease as the result of electronic–conformational interactions, as shown schematically in Fig. 31. The motion of the electron is enhanced by conformational changes (see Chapter 6).

What makes respiration possible? What determines the energy balance of a living system? These problems are treated generally in the next chapter. Here we will say only that the existence of a living system depends on nutrition. The final source of animal nourishment is plants, and plants accumulate energy emitted by the sun.

Photosynthesis is a totality of processes even more complicated than the respiration chain. The processes of photosynthesis are localized in the membranes of chloroplasts, the subcellular organelles in the leaves of green plants. The total process of photosynthesis consists of the electron transfer from a donor such as water, toward an acceptor, such as carbon dioxide:

$$DH_2 + A \xrightarrow{\text{light}} D + AH_2$$

Here DH_2 is the donor and A the acceptor of electrons or of hydrogen atoms. This process proceeds under the action of light, which supplies the system with the necessary energy. In contrast to the respiratory chain, the flow of electrons in the photosynthetic chain from donor to acceptor proceeds in the direction opposite to that of falling oxidative–reductive potential. Hence, the process requires

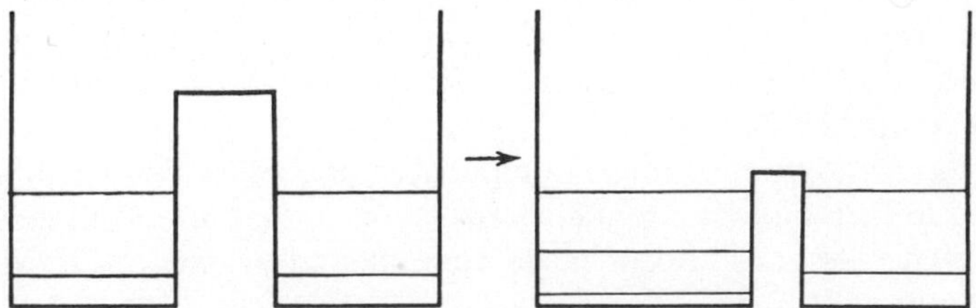

Fig. 31 Change of the barrier due to ECI.

energy. In the course of photosynthesis, oxygen is produced as well as complicated organic substances, such as the carbohydrate hexose ($n = 6$):

$$n\,H_2O + nCO_2 \xrightarrow{\text{light}} (CH_2O)_n + nO_2$$

The light is absorbed in chlorophyll molecules, which are responsible for the green color of plants, and in other pigment molecules. The transformation of the energy of absorbed light into the energy of electrons and then into the energy of chemical bonds proceeds in a very complicated set of reactions in which a series of enzymes participate. As the result of photosynthesis, energy is stored in the organic substances of plants. Simultaneously, oxygen produced from water is given off into the atmosphere.

During the transmission of the electronic flow along the photosynthetic chain, the phosphorylation of ADP occurs, using a fraction of the absorbed light energy. We cannot say that the physics of photosynthesis is totally elucidated, but a series of problems related to photosynthesis has been solved by science.

The study of photosynthesis is of practical importance in agriculture and energetics. There is hope that as a result of these studies, batteries that accumulate solar energy will be constructed. Up to now the most effective method of accumulating solar energy has been photosynthesis. Today, we can suggest nothing better than growing plants such as sunflower or sugar cane, which give large amounts of wood mass (cellulose) rapidly, and using this mass and the products of its dry rectification as fuel. Of course, the effectivity here is low.

More detailed information about photosynthesis will be found in the books [14, 19].

Photosynthesis is not the only biological phenomenon determined by the action of light. A second such phenomenon is vision. We now have a clear picture of the molecular processes occurring under the action of the light absorbed in the functional molecules of rhodopsin. These molecules are localized in the specific membranes of the cells forming the eye's retina. Rhodopsin is a complex of the protein opsin with the retinal molecule, which contains a sequence of conjugated π-bonds. Under the action of light quanta, the rhodopsin splits into opsin and retinal. The retinal then undergoes a conformational transition that uses a large amount of light energy because the bonds are conjugated and the internal rotation around them is strongly hindered. It is not clear yet how these photochemical events cause the appearance of the nervous impulses and of the picture in the brain.

In all the bioenergetic processes described here, the determining role belongs to specialized membranes. A short list of the properties of bioenergetic membranes is presented in Table IV (according to Witt).

In Table IV $h\nu$ means the light absorption; $\Delta\psi$ the change of electric potential; i the electric (ionic) current; e the transport of electrons; ATP (+) phosphorylation, the synthesis of ATP; ATP (−) the hydrolysis of ATP and consumption of the liberated energy.

We have already considered the "charging of the accumulator," that is, the synthesis of ATP. As mentioned earlier, the energy of ATP is spent on protein biosynthesis and active transport. Another important use of the chemical energy of ATP is its transformation into mechanical work.

Life cannot exist without mechanical motion at every level of biological organization. Cells and intracellular organelles move; organisms grow and move. These motions mean the performance of much mechanical work—let us remember the achievements of an athlete or the jumps of a flea. This work is performed under conditions of constant temperature and pressure; hence its source cannot be thermal energy. There can be no source of mechanical work in living nature other than chemical energy.

Of course the work of a steam engine or of an internal combustion engine also occurs on account of chemical energy—the burning of fuel is the chemical reaction of oxidation. However, in these cases chemical energy is first transformed into thermal energy, and only later is the thermal energy transformed into mechanical work—with big losses. The chemical properties and the structure of fuel are not important here; the high heat productivity of the fuel is what counts. For an engine to work, there must be a difference in temperatures, that is, a heater and a cooler must be present. It is clear that

TABLE IV

PROPERTIES OF BIOENERGETIC MEMBRANES

Photosynthesis	$h\nu$	$\Delta\psi$	i	e	ATP (+ and −)
Respiration	—	$\Delta\psi$	i	e	ATP (+ and −)
Vision	$h\nu$	$\Delta\psi$	i	—	ATP (−)
Nerves	—	$\Delta\psi$	i	—	ATP (−)
Muscles	—	$\Delta\psi$	i	—	ATP (−)

biomechanics has nothing in common with these processes—here chemical energy is transformed directly into mechanical work; there is no thermal stage. How can such a mechanochemical process be performed?

The contractile fibrillar proteins serve as the working substances of the biological mechanochemical systems. At first it was suggested that work is done as a result of the folding and unfolding of the polymeric chains because of their electrostatic properties. Proteins are polyelectrolytes; they contain amino acidic residues, which can have positive or negative charges at the R groups. The residues Arg and Lys, for example, can be positively charged, and the residues Glu and Asp negatively.

Let us imagine a polymeric chain. Residues with charges of the same sign repel each other, and therefore the chain becomes elongated. If the charges are compensated by small ions, the mutual repulsion vanishes and the chain becomes folded in a coil because of the conformational motility of its links as a result of internal rotations around single bonds.

Such processes have been realized. In a model mechanochemical engine constructed by Kachalsky and Oplatka, the polyelectrolytic fiber (collagen) submerges alternately into salt solution and into pure water (Fig. 32). In the salt solution the fiber contracts; in water it becomes elongated again. The engine works continuously, and it can lift the load till the moment when, as the result of transfer of ions by the fiber into water, the concentrations in both reservoirs become equal.

This is a beautiful experiment, but biological contractile systems work otherwise. The cross-striated muscle is the best studied biological mechanochemical system. Three groups of facts concerning muscular contraction are known: first, information about the struc-

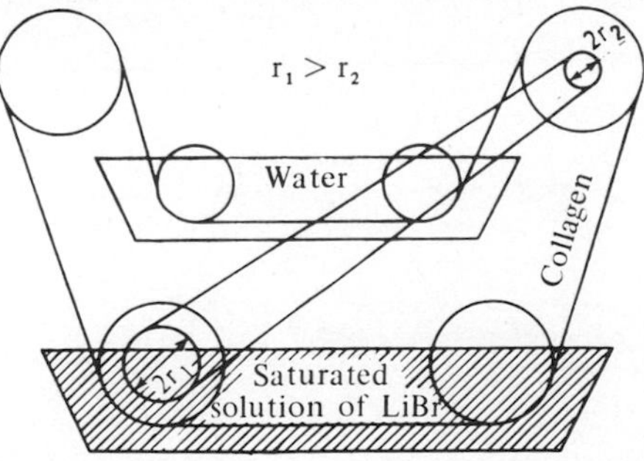

Fig. 32 The mechanochemical engine.

tural changes in the contracting muscular fiber obtained with the help of the electron microscope and x-ray diffraction; second, information about the biochemical processes in muscle; and third, the results of direct measurements of the mechanical and thermal properties of muscle. Electronic microscopy shows that the cross-striated muscle is formed by thin fibers—myofibrils—and they are arranged in a complicated but very regular structure. The myofibrils are built by thin and thick protein threads, known respectively as actin and myosin. The thin threads contain also regulatory proteins, such as tropomyosin, troponine, and actinine. Bridges are formed between the thin and thick threads. During contraction of the fiber, the threads slide in relation to each other and the muscle contracts like a field glass. This is shown schematically in Fig. 33. The "sliding model" of muscular contraction was suggested and confirmed in the works of Huxley, Hanson, and others.

The main biochemical process occurring in muscle was discovered in 1939 by Engelhardt and Ljubimova. They showed that myosin acts as an enzyme (ATPase), splitting ATP. During ATP splitting, energy is liberated. Now it is clear that the mutual shift of the protein threads and the pulling or pushing force can be produced only by conformational changes occurring in contractile proteins, that is, in the threads or bridges formed between them. The molecular mechanism by which the chemical energy released during the dephosphorylation of ATP is transformed into the energy of conformational motion remains unknown. Here we meet again with electronic–conformational interactions, that is, the transformation of the electronic energy of ATP into the conformational energy of proteins. Mechanochemistry is directly connected with enzymatic activity and evidently cannot exist without it.

It has been established that the nervous impulse is the cause of electrochemical processes in muscle. They begin by the appearance

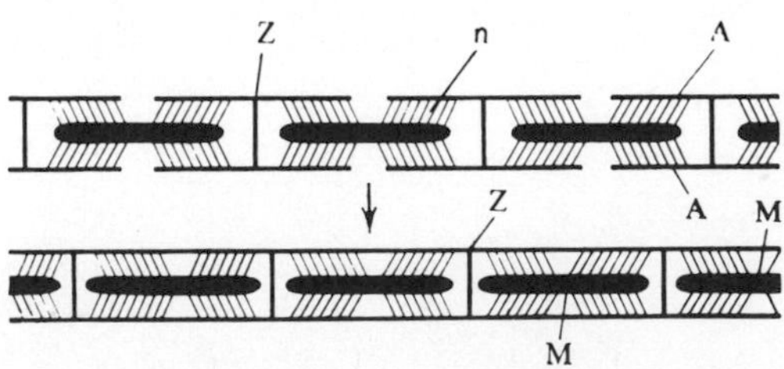

Fig. 33 Shortening of the muscle fiber. Z, membranes; A, thin threads of actin; M, thick threads of myosin; and n, bridges.

of the Ca^{2+} ions in the liquid medium surrounding the protein threads. The Ca^{2+} ions are necessary for the functioning of actomyosin, for it closes the bridges between the thick and thin protein threads.

The mechanical properties of the muscle were studied in detail by Hill, who established the fundamental equation connecting the velocity of the muscle shortening with the stress applied by the load P. Hill's equation is valid for comparatively small changes of the muscle length. For steady shortening with a constant velocity V, the equation has the form

$$(P + a)V = b(P_0 - P) \tag{52}$$

Here a and b are constants, and P_0 is the maximum load that can be supported by the muscle without it shortening or lengthening (if $P = P_0$, $V = 0$). For the sartorius muscle of the frog, $a \cong 0.25P_0$. The dependence of V on P is hyperbolic. At $P = 0$, the velocity of shortening is maximal:

$$\begin{aligned} V_{\max} &= \frac{b}{a} P_0 \\ &\cong 4b \end{aligned} \tag{53}$$

The constant b depends strongly on temperature; it doubles if the muscle is heated by 10° (in the region of physiological temperatures).

The empirical equation (52) has a very simple form. We may think that it expresses some relatively simple regularity. Really, this equation can be obtained by the theory based on the sliding model shown in Fig. 33. The pulling effort is produced as a result of the closing and subsequent opening of the bridges between the thick and thin protein threads. Let the number of the possible bridges in a sarcomere—the part of the fiber between Z-membranes to which the thin threads are attached (Fig. 33)—be n_0. Hence the maximum load that can be maintained by the muscle, or the maximum stress developed by it, is

$$P_0 = n_0 f_0 \tag{54}$$

where f_0 is the force developed by one bridge. Similarly, the applied force can be expressed in the form

$$P = n_0 f \tag{55}$$

where f is the external force per bridge. At any given moment, under the load P, not all n_0 bridges are working; only a smaller number n of them are.

Hence

$$\frac{n}{n_0} = w$$
$$\leq 1 \qquad (56)$$

The ratio w is equal to 1 only at $P = P_0$, when all bridges are working.

The closing and opening of the bridge means the presence in the system of the force of friction, which is proportional to the velocity of shortening. Now we can write the balance of forces using Newton's second law

$$m\dot{V} = P' - P - \gamma V \qquad (57)$$

where m is some mass, $\dot{V}$ is the acceleration, P' the force developed by the bridges, and γV the friction force. Under stationary conditions, the acceleration $\dot{V}$ is equal to zero. Both P' and γV are proportional to the number n of working bridges. Calculating for one bridge, we get Eq. (57) in the form

$$nf_0 - n_0 f - n\beta v = 0 \qquad (58)$$

where v is the rate of shortening of one sarcomere, and $\beta = \gamma/n$ is the coefficient of friction due to one bridge. It follows from Eq. (58) that

$$v = \frac{1}{\beta}\left(f_0 - \frac{f}{w}\right) \qquad (59)$$

The value of w [Eq. (56)] depends on the force f. The most simple and natural guess is that w depends linearly on f, that is,

$$w(f) = A + Bf \qquad (60)$$

If $f = f_0$, $w = 1$ and $f = 0$ when the rate of shortening is maximal, then $w = \tau < 1$ is the smallest fraction of working bridges. We get the values of A and B:

$$1 = A + Bf_0$$
$$\tau = A$$

and

$$w = 1 + (1 - \tau)\frac{f}{f_0} \qquad (61)$$

Putting Eq. (61) into Eq. (59), after simple transformations we get

$$v = \frac{f_0}{\beta}\frac{\tau}{1-\tau}\frac{f_0 - f}{f + \frac{\tau}{1-\tau}f_0} \tag{62}$$

This equation is similar to Hill's equation (52), in which (in calculation per sarcomere)

$$\begin{aligned} a &= \frac{\tau}{1-\tau}f_0 \\ b &= \frac{\tau}{1-\tau}\frac{f_0}{\beta} \end{aligned} \tag{63}$$

At $a \cong 0.25 f_0$, $\tau \cong 0.2$. We get also that at $f = 0$,

$$v_{\mathrm{max}} = \frac{f_0}{\beta} \tag{64}$$

This calculation shows that Hill's equation describes the plastic flow—the motion of the protein threads with friction. The equation does not contain elasticity. The strong dependence of the constant b on temperature is determined by the natural dependence of the friction coefficient on temperature. Further theoretical analysis allows us to express b by molecular constants connecting this quantity with the energy of activation necessary for the dephosphorylation of ATP [19].

Many difficulties must be overcome along the way to understanding heat production during muscular contraction. The muscle works like an electric motor. The bigger is the load in the network, the greater is the current consumed by the motor. The bigger is the load lifted by the muscle, the greater is the power developed by it, and simultaneously the greater is the heat produced by the muscle. One thing is clear: both the work of the muscle and the evolved heat are derived from one source—the energy of ATP.

Notwithstanding the enormous number of books and papers devoted to muscular contraction, we are far from constructing an artificial device that works like a muscle. This would be very tempting—the efficiency of the muscles of some animals reaches 75%.

More detailed information about the physics of muscular contraction can be found in the literature [19, 21].

We end this chapter with a few words about the flight muscles of insects. They perform many contractions in a second—everybody has heard the buzzing of mosquitoes. It has been established that the frequency of contraction of insect muscles surpasses the frequency of the arrival of the nervous impulse by hundreds of times. In other words, we meet here with a clear case of an autooscillatory process. Its investigation is a fascinating problem of biophysics, as is the study of nonstationary contractions of the muscles of vertebrates.

By considering muscular contraction, we have seen the role of experimental and theoretical physics in the studies of the biological (bioenergetic) processes.

CHAPTER 9

Thermodynamics and Information Theory in Biology

We have already been acquainted with various areas of molecular biophysics and biophysics of cells. Of course they are presented here only as a short account with a single goal—to give the reader a general introduction to these areas.

Now we can return to the main problems of the connection between physics and biology.

Physics has two approaches to the phenomena it studies. The first approach is phenomenological; the most general regularities are studied without consideration of the detailed nature of the phenomena. The second approach is atomic–molecular; it aims to uncover the elementary basis of phenomena and to determine their quantitative characteristics. Phenomenological theory says what can exist; atomic–molecular theory describes what does exist. Of course there is no contradiction between these two approaches.

We have spoken till now mainly about the atomic–molecular approach to investigation. Now we shall consider a general phenomenological theory: thermodynamics.

In the nineteenth century, two great evolutionary theories were expounded—Darwin's theory of biological evolution and the theory of evolution of an isolated physical system, formulated by the second law of thermodynamics. The second law was discovered and its theoretical foundation explored by Carnot, Clausius, Boltzmann, and Gibbs.

In the final analysis, all fields of natural sciences are interconnected; moreover, human culture develops as a united whole. Not only the biologists but also the physicists of the nineteenth century met with the problem of evolution; the studies connected with the second law of thermodynamics were devoted to the irreversible evolution of a physical system.

According to the second law, an isolated physical system (that is, a system that has no exchange of energy and substance with the external world) tends spontaneously and irreversibly toward the state of equilibrium characterized by maximal disorder (maximal entropy). One example of this law is the transfer of heat from a warmer to a cooler body, but not the reverse. In equilibrium, the temperatures become equal. Another example is diffusion. Suppose a vessel is divided in two equal parts by a partition, and initially one part contains gas and another part is empty. After the partition is removed, gas will diffuse into the whole vessel, and both halves will contain an equal average number of molecules. The reverse process—accumulation of molecules in one half of the vessel—does not occur. In both examples, the system was ordered in the beginning: the temperatures of the two bodies were different, and gas was present in one half of the vessel. The final state is disordered: the temperatures or the number of molecules became equal. The measure of disorder is entropy, which, according to Boltzmann, is expressed by the formula

$$S = k \ln \Gamma \tag{65}$$

where $k = 1.38 \times 10^{-16}$ erg/grad is Boltzmann's constant and Γ is the statistical weight of the given state, that is, the number of ways of realizing the state. Let us explain the significance of this quantity with the help of a simple example.

Imagine a vessel divided in two halves and containing only four molecules. In Fig. 34, the possible distributions of these molecules and the statistical weights of these distributions are shown. Distributions 1 and 5 have the smallest probability, as every one of them can be realized in only one way. The probabilities of states 2 and 4 are four times higher as each can be realized in four ways. For example, in case 2 the distributions of the numerated molecules are 1,234; 2,134; 3,124; 4,123. Finally, the uniform distribution 3 has the highest probability; it can be realized in six ways: 12,34; 13,24; 14,23; 34,12; 24,13; 23,14. The entropy is maximal for this distribution.

However, this maximum of entropy is not sharp if the number of molecules is small—distribution 3 is only 50% more probable than

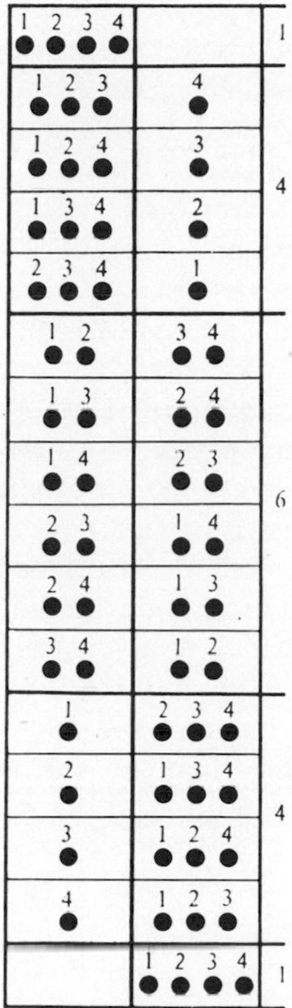

Fig. 34 The distribution of four molecules in a vessel divided into two equal parts.

distributions 2 and 4, and hence the four molecules in our example can possess nonmaximal entropy with a high probability. In contrast, if the number of molecules is big, for example, 1000, then the distribution 498,502 will have some probability, but the probability of the distribution 333,667 will be extremely small. This means that the second law has a probabilistic, statistical character. It is valid for the average, and its precision is higher the greater is the number of particles contained in the system. We cannot consider the possibility of accumulating the entire thousand molecules in one half of the vessel as nonexistent, but the probability of such an event is vanishingly small. At the same time, small deviations from the averaged behavior—fluctuations—occur always; and, of course, the relative role of fluctuations increases sharply as the number of particles in the vessel decreases.

Thus an isolated physical system evolves toward its most probable disordered state with maximal entropy. The path of biological evolution is reversed—it goes from the simplest unicellular organisms—bacteria—toward multicellular ones, including man. Evolution tends from simplicity toward complexity in the direction of increasing order. We wonder whether there is a contradiction between the physical and biological evolution.

This contradiction is imaginary. A living organism is an open system, and the law of maximum entropy is valid only for an isolated system. In an open system, entropy can grow, remain constant, or diminish, depending on the amount of entropy produced inside the system, inflowing from outside, or outflowing into the external world. If we want to determine the thermodynamic balance of a living organism, we must investigate an isolated system containing this organism and the feeding substances, water and air. A good model of such a system is a spaceship with astronauts.

Of course, the second law of thermodynamics is valid for an isolated system that contains a living organism. The entropy of the whole system increases because the entropy of substances excreted by the organism is higher than the entropy of the nourishing substances. As Schrödinger wrote, an organism feeds on negative entropy [9].

An astronaut is an open system. The change of its entropy is a sum of two fractions: entropy production due to the processes occurring inside the organism d_iS, and inflow or outflow (exchange) of entropy d_eS

$$dS = d_iS + d_eS \tag{66}$$

The quantity d_iS is positive, and remains also in the conditions of the astronaut isolated. The sign of d_eS depends on the circumstances. Expression (66) shows that a nonequilibrium but stationary state is possible in an open system characterized by constant total entropy:

$$\begin{aligned} S &= \text{const} \\ dS &= 0 \\ d_eS &= -d_iS \end{aligned} \tag{67}$$

In this case, the production of entropy inside the system is compensated by its outflow into the surrounding medium. An organism can be maintained in a stationary but nonequilibrium state. A healthy young man, whose growth is already completed, remains in such a state for a rather long time with no change in his mass. Of course when a child is growing or an adult is aging, the state of the organism is no longer stationary.

The difference between the equilibrium state of an isolated system and the stationary state of an open system can be explained with the help of a simple model (Fig. 35). The flow of liquid from one vessel into another represents the kinetic process considered, such as the chemical reaction. If the system is closed and the liquid does not flow into the vessels from outside and does not outflow (Fig. 35a), then, with a velocity determined by the opening of the cock, the whole liquid will flow into the lower vessel, and equilibrium will be established. The level of liquid in the lower vessel represents the equilibrium state of reaction.

If the system is open, nonequilibrium levels of liquid will be established in the upper and lower vessels (Fig 35b). In this case the level will depend on the opening of the cock. The cock is a model for the catalyst—the substance that does not participate in the final reaction but that influences its rate. In a closed system, the final result of reaction process does not depend on its rate or on the opening of the cock. Finally the constant level of liquid in the lower vessel becomes established. In an open system, not only the rate but also the degree of proceeding of reaction is dependent on the catalyst.

The usual thermodynamics is in reality thermostatics—it studies only equilibrium states and does not consider the problems of kinetics. Time is not contained in thermodynamic expressions. However, in the studies of open systems in nonequilibrium states, we

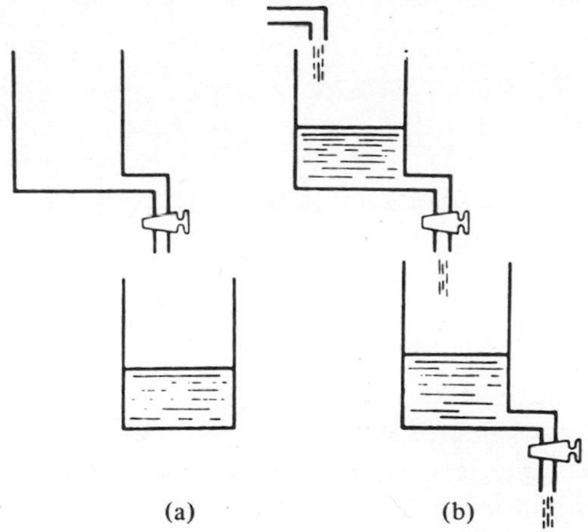

Fig. 35 A thermodynamic system: (a) closed; (b) open.

encounter the problem of the rate of change of the system's state, in particular the rate of entropy production. The production of entropy per unit volume of the system is called the dissipation function. We have

$$\frac{d_iS}{dt} = \int \sigma \, dV \geq 0 \tag{68}$$

The dissipation function σ is positive. Thermodynamics shows that σ for the nonequilibrium system near equilibrium (the quantitative criterion for this neighborhood can be formulated) can be represented by the sum of products of the so-called generalized flows J_i and generalized forces X_i:

$$\sigma = \sum_i J_i X_i \geq 0 \tag{69}$$

What are the generalized flows and forces? In the case of electric conductivity, the flow is the electrical current and the force is the difference of potentials; in the case of heat conductivity, the flow is the heat flow and the generalized force is proportional to the difference of temperatures. Corresponding expressions can be written for chemical reactions. Near equilibrium, the flows depend linearly on forces, and vice versa. For example, electric current is proportional to voltage according to Ohm's law. Let there be two flows—the flow of heat, J_1, and the diffusional flow of the mass, J_2—and two generalized forces—difference of temperatures, X_1, and difference of concentrations, X_2

$$\begin{aligned} J_1 &= L_{11}X_1 + L_{12}X_2 \\ J_2 &= L_{21}X_1 + L_{22}X_2 \end{aligned} \tag{70}$$

Both flows depend on both forces; they are coupled. Near equilibrium, as Onsager has shown, the phenomenological coupling coefficients are symmetric:

$$L_{12} = L_{21} \tag{71}$$

The coupling of flows means that the single flows that are impossible because they are connected with the increase of free energy become possible at the expense of other forces. Thus, for instance if the product of flow and force J_1X_1 is negative, then because of the second positive addendum J_2X_2 the flow J_1 can be realized. Only the summary condition (69) must be fulfilled, that is,

$$J_1X_1 + J_2X_2 > 0 \tag{72}$$

and in the case $J_1X_1 < 0$ we must have

$$J_2X_2 > |J_1X_1| \tag{73}$$

We have met with such relationships already. In active transport across membranes, the diffusional flow of ions is coupled with the enzymatic reaction of ATP splitting. In biosynthesis of protein, the polycondensation of amino acids is coupled with the hydrolysis of ATP.

Thus we see that linear nonequilibrium thermodynamics, which is valid near equilibrium, explains very important features of the open systems—the coupling of flows and the appearance of stationary nonequilibrium states.

The stationary nonequilibrium state that is near equilibrium is characterized by the minimal entropy production, that is, the minimum of the dissipation function σ. This is Prigogine's theorem. Linear thermodynamics is treated in a series of monographs [10, 14, 19, 22, 23].

Can linear thermodynamics describe the development of a biological system? Development means the increase of ordering, that is, the decrease of entropy. Evidently, the open system can develop if the outflow of entropy into the surrounding medium exceeds the production of entropy inside the system. However, near equilibrium development is impossible. It can be shown that a system shifted from a stationary state near equilibrium returns to this state monotonically, without oscillations, according to exponential law. Near equilibrium, any enzyme catalyzes both the direct and the reverse reactions.

Let us imagine the process of ordering in an initially homogeneous disordered system. Ordering is possible even if the system is not only nonequilibrium but far from equilibrium. Under these conditions, the relations (69) and (70) are not fulfilled—the flows cannot be represented as linear functions of forces. For the spontaneous transition of a system from a random into an ordered state, it is necessary for the random, disordered state to be unstable. Such a situation is found in an open chemical system of autocatalytic reactions, such as

$$A + X \rightleftarrows 2X$$

$$B + X \rightleftarrows C$$

where X is some intermediate. The quantity of X increases in the first autocatalytic reaction as the result of interaction of this substance itself with substance *A*. The summary reaction is

$$A + B \rightleftarrows C$$

Thermodynamics allows us to formulate only the general conditions of stability or instability that determine the possibility of order appearing in the open system [19, 22, 23]. A thorough theoretical investigation of such processes does not belong to thermodynamics; it requires the analysis of concrete kinetic mechanisms. Nonlinear thermodynamics is in reality kinetics.

Both theoretical and experimental studies have been made of model systems in which behavior regularly ordered in space and time occurs in spite of the disordered, homogeneous initial state of the system. First, we must speak about oscillatory and wave processes in chemistry. It is necessary to emphasize that undamped oscillations are possible only in a system that is far from equilibrium. We know that oscillations occur at all levels of structure of the biological system, beginning with the daily rhythms of living phenomena and ending with the oscillatory reactions of enzymes. We speak of "biological clocks." All of this demonstrates the remoteness of biological systems from equilibrium. Equilibrium means death.

In 1958, Belousov observed for the first time a periodic chemical reaction in a homogeneous oxidative–reductive system containing bromate, organic acid, and ions of cerium, which can exist in the trivalent and tetravalent states:

$$Ce^{4+} + \text{electron} \rightleftarrows Ce^{3+}$$

The experiment is very beautiful. The ions Ce^{4+} and Ce^{3+} have different colors. A few drops of some substance are added to the vessel containing sky-blue liquid. The liquid becomes pink. Then it becomes blue again, then pink; the color of the liquid changes periodically, with thousands of periods. (In the first work of Belousov, the number of periods was small.) Later, Zhabotinsky performed fundamental experimental and theoretical investigations of chemical oscillations in a series of systems. He was able to observe the appearance of leading centers of vibrations and of circular and helical waves. One of the pictures obtained in these works is shown in Fig. 36. It has been established that these reactions are autocatalytic, and the system as a whole is a dissipative system remote from equilib-

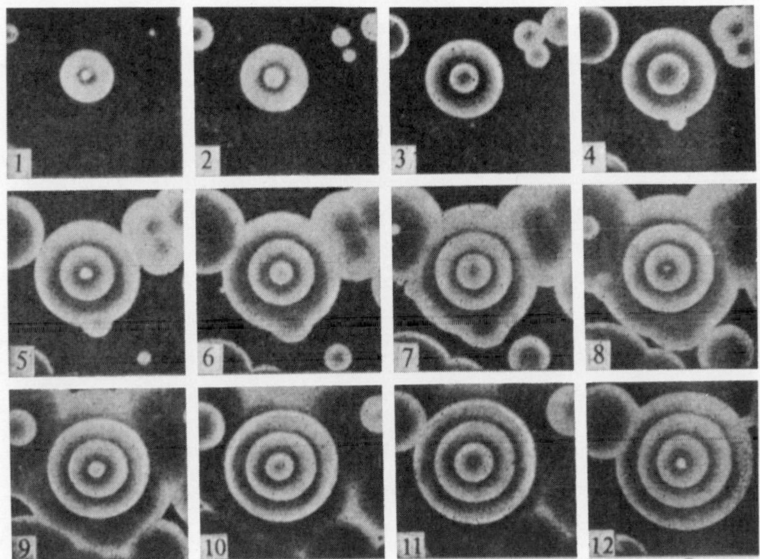

Fig. 36 The leading centers of chemical autooscillations. The numbers are sequential pictures.

rium. A detailed description of the results obtained is contained in Zhabotinsky's monograph [19, 24, 25].

One would think that these beautiful phenomena are interesting for chemistry but not for biology. This is erroneous. Of course biological systems are much more complicated; but the aim of physics and all theoretical natural science is the discovery of fundamental laws. This aim requires simplified models; oscillatory chemical processes serve as a model of biological processes. This model also helps us approach medical problems. It is known that in some pathological states, the heart goes from regular periodic work to fibrillation, irregular random contractions leading to death. The study of the heart tissue as a nonequilibrium excitable medium similar in some respects to the chemical oscillating system was performed by Krinsky. His work laid the foundation for investigating the phenomena of fibrillation and establishing those physicochemical parameters of the system that must be influenced for defibrillation of the heart, that is, for the restoration of its normal functioning [19, 24, 25].

Information theory is directly connected with thermodynamics.

In contrast to the popular concept of information as a totality of data contained in some message, the word "information" has a rigorous quantitative sense in science. Let us throw a die. The probability of obtaining any particular result from the possible six is $\frac{1}{6}$. If two dice are thrown, the amount of information obtained is two times greater than with one die; but the probability of the definite result of throwing two dice is equal to the product of probabilities of throwing the first and the second die, $\frac{1}{6} \times \frac{1}{6} = \frac{1}{36}$. Hence, the pieces of information are added while the probabilities multiply. This means that information depends logarithmically on the probability of the given event W or on the inverse quantity—the number of possibilities of equal probability Γ, from which only one possibility is chosen.

$$I = -K \log W \tag{74}$$

or

$$I = K \log \Gamma \tag{75}$$

In these formulas, the coefficient K and hence the base of the logarithm remain uncertain. The coefficient K can be chosen in a most convenient way. It is accepted that $K = 1$ and the base of the logarithm is 2. In this case,

$$\begin{aligned} I &= -\log_2 W \\ &= \log_2 \Gamma \end{aligned} \tag{76}$$

Evidently we get $I = 1$ if $W = \frac{1}{2}$ or $\Gamma = 2$. In other words, the unit of information, called a "bit" (binary digit), is obtained when the choice is performed of one of two equiprobable possibilities. Throwing a die, we obtain the information

$$\begin{aligned} I &= -\log_2 \frac{1}{6} \\ &= \log_2 6 \\ &= 2.58 \text{ bits.} \end{aligned}$$

Using formula (76), the amount of information in a text can be calculated. Thus, the DNA chain containing N links can have 4^N various primary structures because this text is written with the help of the four letter alphabet. Only one definite sequence from 4^N exists, and we get

$$\begin{aligned} I &= -\log_2 \frac{1}{4^N} \\ &= \log_2 4^N \\ &= 2N \text{ bits.} \end{aligned}$$

What is the relationship of these calculations to thermodynamics?

Formula (76) is similar to formula (65), which connects the entropy S with the number Γ of ways of realizing some given state of a statistical system. We can connect I and S, identifying Γ in both expressions. Then

$$\begin{aligned} S &= k \ln \Gamma \\ &= Ik \ln 2 \\ &= \frac{1}{\log_2 e} kI \end{aligned} \tag{77}$$

or numerically

$$\begin{aligned} S &\cong 10^{-16} I \text{ erg/grad} \\ &\cong 2.3 \times 10^{-24} I \text{ cal/grad} \end{aligned} \tag{78}$$

Here I is expressed in bits.

However, this is not an exact analogy. We pay for the obtained information with an increase of entropy. It is impossible to obtain information about an adiabatically isolated system whose entropy remains unchanged. Let a liquid be frozen in a vessel. Entropy decreases and information increases because the molecules that have been distributed at random in the liquid are now located in the crystal in a definite way. However, it is impossible to freeze a liquid without a refrigerator, which is heated in this process and its entropy increased. According to the second law of thermodynamics, the entropy of the total system will increase.

We can say that entropy is the measure of the lack of information about a system. The equivalence of information and entropy is to some extent similar to Einstein's law

$$E = mc^2$$

which formulates the equivalence of mass and energy, physical quantities measured by different units. We can write a conservation law

$$S + I = \text{const} \tag{79}$$

Increase of S means decrease of I, and vice versa. Thus we can express I in entropical units (e.u.), that is, in calories per degree, and S in bits; S is the measure of disorder, I, the measure of order.

According to Eq. (78), a great number of bits is equivalent to a very small entropy; the value of the bit in entropical units is very cheap. Sometimes the literature contrasts the flow of information with the flow of energy. Actually, information can be transmitted only in real physical processes, but with small changes of energy and entropy.

We also meet with the concept of the "antientropicity" of cells and organisms. This word is usually understood as denoting the very high degree of order in the living system. Monod wrote that the difference between the living system and nonliving crystal is the much greater orderliness in the organism [26]. This is wrong. Let us consider a simple calculation made by Blumenfeld [14].

Let us calculate the orderliness of the structure of an organism formed by cells. The human body contains $\sim 10^{13}$ cells. If all of them were different (actually they are not), then for a unique distribution of cells we would get

$$\begin{aligned} I &= \log_2(10^{13}!) \\ &\cong 10^{13} \log_2 10^{13} \\ &\cong 10^{14} \text{ bits} \end{aligned}$$

which is equivalent to 10^{-9} e.u.

A cell contains approximately 10^8 biopolymer molecules. If all of them are different, and their distribution in the cell is unique, we get

$$\begin{aligned} I &= \log(10^8!) \\ &\cong 10^8 \log_2 10^8 \\ &\cong 2.6 \times 10^9 \text{ bits} \end{aligned}$$

and for all cells

$$\begin{aligned} I &\cong 10^{13} \times 2.6 \times 10^9 \\ &\cong 2.6 \times 10^{22} \text{ bits,} \end{aligned}$$

that is, 6×10^{-2} e.u.

The human organism contains approximately 7 kg of protein and 150 g of DNA, corresponding to 3×10^{25} amino acid residues and 3×10^{23} nucleotides. The unique distribution of all these monomeric links corresponds to $I = 1.3 \times 10^{26}$ bits for proteins and 6×10^{23} bits for DNA, which is equivalent to 300 and 1.4 e.u. The decrease of entropy in the formation of an organism is not more than 301.5 e.u., which corresponds to the change of entropy at the condensation of 170 g of water vapor—a very small quantity. In this respect an organism lacks any specific orderliness; its order does not differ from that in a piece of rock of the same mass.

There are, however, important differences between the crystal and the organism. The amount of information in them can be equal, but its character is different. The crystal contains repeated, redundant information, that is, the crystal is periodic; the elementary cell of the crystalline lattice is repeated many times. An organism, in contrast, is an aperiodic crystal with a large amount of nonredundant information.

This does not exhaust the difference between crystals and organisms. It has been emphasized many times in this book that the organism is an open system, a specific chemical machine working on the basis of balanced weak and strong interactions, which provide direct connection and feedback. Moreover, the machine has a complicated, functional structure. The behavior of such a machine depends on the position and state of every constituent element. Hence the living system is not a statistical system like gas or a periodic crystal.

Cells and organisms are dynamic systems. Their description in terms of entropy is not sufficient, for such a description is lawful but it does not explain the workings of a dynamic system. Let us consider a simple example brought by Blumenfeld.

An engine contains a cylinder with a piston. Both are made of metal, and it is possible to calculate the entropy of these parts. If we extract the piston from the cylinder, the entropy will not change much—but the engine will not work.

In an analogous way, we can calculate the amount of information and the corresponding amount of entropy in the biopolymers of the cell. However, this does not give us any understanding of the properties of biological molecules. It is not the amount of information in DNA that is important but the program of the protein synthesis contained in its text. In other words, for biology, it is not the amount of information that is of importance but its content, its value for the programmed process. We shall speak about the value of information in Chapter 12.

Of course, the laws of thermodynamics are valid both in nonliving and in living nature; but to understand life phenomena we need another physics, such as is developing now in systems theory and automatic regulation theory. There will be no new physical principles that differ from those already established. However, the study of "machine" systems is new, and it will lead to the expansion of physical concepts and the formation of physics of specific dynamic systems—chemical, molecular ones.

The relationship between dynamics and statistics is very complicated. In a steam engine the statistical part—water vapor—is structurally and functionally separated from the dynamic part—metallic engine components. In a biological system, dynamics and statistics are combined. The organism is an aperiodic crystal, that is, a heterogeneous, nonuniform, but ordered system. This definition relates also to individual functional parts of the organism—to the organs, tissues, cells, and single protein globules. However, a globule preserves some conformational motility; it possesses statistical elements that perform dynamic roles.

Physics approaches the complicated problems of biological development from a different perspective. One method of investigation uses the physicomathematical modeling treated in the next chapter. The unification of different approaches into a theoretical biology, is a task of the future; but the work in these fields is proceeding, and has already begun to yield very important and interesting results.

CHAPTER 10

Physicomathematical Modeling of Biological Processes

The use of mathematics in studies of biological processes, as in economics, shows that it is possible to treat the subject quantitatively; it has nothing to do with physics. Complicated calculations of dynamics of populations belong to zoology or botany, but not to biophysics.

However, if the basis of the mathematical model is a physical concept, we can consider such a model as a biophysical one. Such modeling is the method used in developing the biophysics of complicated systems [19, 23–25, 27, 28].

Nevertheless, as an initial example we shall consider not a physical but a zoological model: the "predator–prey" model suggested and investigated by Volterra [8]. Later it was shown that mathematical models of a series of fundamental processes occurring in cells and organisms have much in common with Volterra's model.

Let us imagine a population of rodents feeding on vegetable food that is in excess. With this population, the population of predators that feeds on rodents interacts. What will be the temporal dynamics of the two populations?

The qualitative answer is quite evident. Let the predator be lynxes and the prey hares. Lynxes kill the hares, and the number of lynxes increases because food is necessary for their reproduction. Simultaneously, the number of hares diminishes. Then the number of lynxes becomes smaller because of the shortage of food. The consequence is the increase of the number of hares, as the probability of their meeting with lynxes becomes smaller. Then the number of lynxes increases again and the number of hares decreases, etc. The numbers of both populations must change periodically with a phase shift. This reasoning is supported by facts. Figure 37 shows the dynamics of populations of hares and lynxes during the years 1845–1935 according to data on the numbers of skins obtained by the Hudson Bay Company.

However, without calculations we cannot establish theoretically the period and amplitude of these changes. Let us make these calculations. Let the number of hares be x and that of lynxes y. The kinetic equations express the rates of changes of x and y as functions of these values. The equations are

$$\begin{aligned} \frac{dx}{dt} &= k_1x - kxy \\ \frac{dy}{dt} &= k'xy - k_2y \end{aligned} \tag{80}$$

where dx/dt, dy/dt are the rates of change of x and y. The term k_1x is the rate of reproduction of hares, which is proportional to their number, and $-kxy$ is the rate of extermination of hares, which is proportional to the product of the number of hares and the number of lynxes, that is, to the frequency of their meetings. It is assumed that there are no other causes of destruction of hares; their death is never natural. A similar term $k'xy$ expresses the rate of reproduction of lynxes, which depends on the amount of obtainable food. The term $-k_2y$ is the rate of destruction of lynxes, which is proportional to their number.

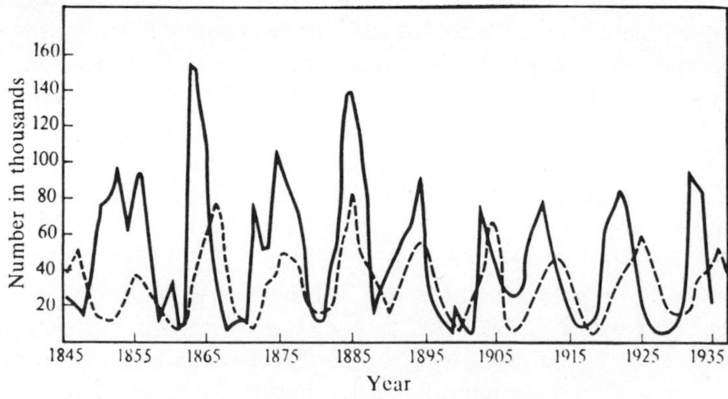

Fig. 37 Changes in lynx and hare populations. Solid line, hare; dashed line, lynx.

The system of equations (80) is nonlinear; their right-hand sides contain the nonlinear products xy. The usual method of investigating such equations is by linearization, that is, the determination of the stationary solutions and the study of small deviations from the stationary state. Such solutions of system (80) do not depend on time, that is, $x_0 = \text{const}$, $y_0 = \text{const}$. Correspondingly,

$$\left(\frac{dx}{dt}\right)_{x=x_0, y=y_0} = \left(\frac{dy}{dt}\right)_{x=x_0, y=y_0} = 0$$

or

$$\begin{aligned} k_1x_0 - kx_0y_0 &= 0 \\ k'x_0y_0 - k_2y_0 &= 0 \end{aligned} \tag{81}$$

It is easily found that

$$\begin{aligned} y_0 &= \frac{k_1}{k} \\ x_0 &= \frac{k_2}{k'} \end{aligned} \tag{82}$$

Now we look for the solutions to system (80) of the form

$$\begin{aligned} x &= x_0 + \alpha \\ y &= y_0 + \beta \end{aligned} \tag{83}$$

where α and β are small in comparison with x_0 and y_0. Using Eqs. (83) and (81), we get from Eqs. (80)

$$\begin{aligned} \frac{d\alpha}{dt} &= k_1\alpha - kx_0\beta - ky_0\alpha - k\alpha\beta \\ \frac{d\beta}{dt} &= k'x_0\beta + k'y_0\alpha + k'\alpha\beta - k_2\beta \end{aligned} \tag{84}$$

We can neglect the terms $k\alpha\beta$ and $k'\alpha\beta$ because they contain the product of two small quantities. The values of x_0 and y_0 were found already in Eqs. (82). We get the linearized system

$$\begin{aligned} \frac{d\alpha}{dt} &= -\frac{kk_2}{k'}\beta \\ \frac{d\beta}{dt} &= \frac{k'k_1}{k}\alpha \end{aligned} \tag{85}$$

We look for solutions to these equations. They are vibrational:

$$\begin{aligned} \alpha &= Ae^{i\omega t} \\ \beta &= Be^{i\omega t} \end{aligned} \tag{86}$$

where $i = \sqrt{-1}$ and $\omega = 2\pi\nu$ is the circular frequency of vibrations. Substituting Eqs. (86) into Eqs. (85) (and using $d[\exp(i\omega t)]/dt = i\omega \exp(i\omega t)$), we get the equations

$$\begin{aligned} Ai\omega e^{i\omega t} + \frac{kk_2}{k'} Be^{i\omega t} &= 0 \\ Bi\omega e^{i\omega t} + \frac{k'k_1}{k} Ae^{i\omega t} &= 0 \end{aligned} \tag{87}$$

Cancelling $\exp(i\omega t)$, we get

$$\begin{aligned} i\omega A + \frac{kk_2}{k'} B &= 0 \\ -\frac{k'k_1}{k} A + i\omega B &= 0 \end{aligned} \tag{88}$$

The condition of compatibility of these equations is the equality of the ratios A/B obtained from the first and second equation. We find that

$$\begin{aligned} \frac{A}{B} &= -\frac{kk_2}{k'} \frac{1}{i\omega} \\ &= i\omega \frac{k}{k'k_1} \end{aligned} \tag{89}$$

and that the circular frequency of vibration of x and y is

$$\omega = \sqrt{k_1 k_2} \tag{90}$$

The amplitudes and phases of vibration of x and y depend on initial conditions.

This is a beautiful example of a nonlinear vibrational system. It is quite natural that this example is studied in detail in the classic text on the physics of vibrations [29] and in various monographs [19, 27, 28].

The visual method of analysis of nonlinear dynamic equations consists of investigating the "phase portrait" of the system. In our case, such a phase portrait is the set of curves on the plane x,y; points moving along these curves represent the motion of the system. The phase portrait of Volterra's system is shown in Fig. 38. The cyclic curves surround a singular point—the center. This point corresponds to the stationary state of the system, and its coordinates are x_0 and y_0. Initial conditions determine the curve of the system's motion. This motion is unstable; introducing additional hares or lynxes from outside into the system transfers the system to another closed curve.

In 1910 and 1920, long before Volterra's work, Lotka described the behavior of the vibrational chemical autocatalytic system with the help of similar equations. At that time it was a purely abstract theory. Nowadays such processes (Belousov–Zhabotinsky reactions) are well studied. Of course the physical meaning of the variables in the models of Volterra and Lotka is quite different: in the first case, it is the population count; in the second, the concentrations of chemical substances. The concentrations are what concern us in biophysical models.

Let us now consider the simplest model of the "switching" of protein synthesis based on regulation of the genes. Jacob and Monod studied the genetic regulatory system—the operon—in a bacterial cell. A set of structural genes responsible for the synthesis of functional proteins is united with the so-called gene regulator and gene operator. The gene regulator is responsible for synthesizing the protein repressor, which acts at the gene operator to suppress the work of all structural genes adjoining the gene operator. If an inductor—a substance which binds the repressor—is introduced, the structural genes are switched on because the repressor no longer acts on the operator. The system gene operator plus structural genes is called the operon. This scheme, which was confirmed experimentally, is

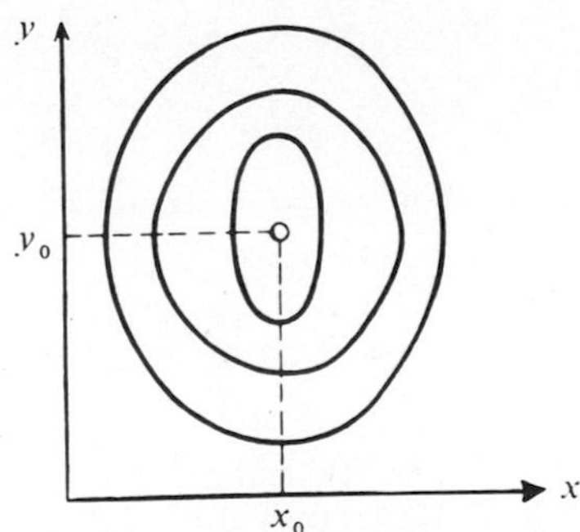

Fig. 38 Phase portrait of the "predator–prey" system.

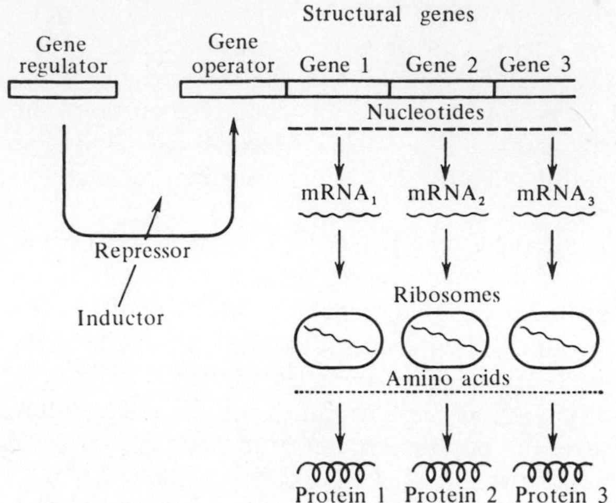

Fig. 39 The scheme of the operon.

shown in Fig. 39. A detailed description can be found in the literature [16, 19, 30].

In the developing cells of a multicellular organism, switching of protein synthesis occurs. At one stage of development a definite set of proteins is synthesized, at another stage another set of proteins. Processes of this kind play a decisive role in cell differentiation.

The simplest model of switching suggested by Jacob and Monad is a system of two operons working crosswise. The schematic pre-

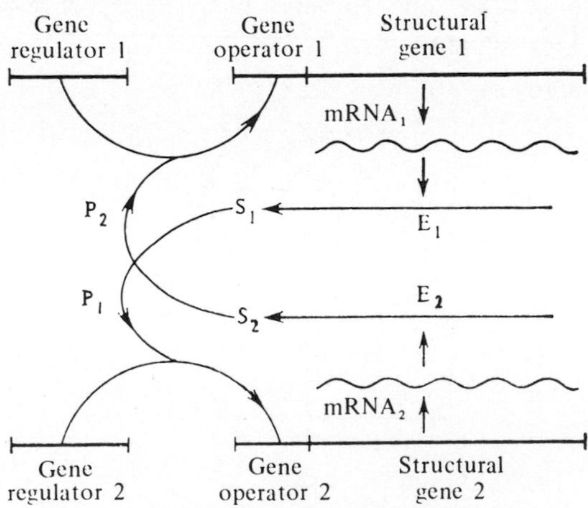

Fig. 40 Two coupled operons.

sentation of such a system is given in Fig. 40. The first operon synthesizes enzyme E_1, which catalyzes the transformation of substrate S_1 into product P_1. This product acts as a corepressor for the second operon, activating its repressor. The second operon synthesizes enzyme E_2, which transforms substrate S_2 into product P_2, activating the repressor of the first operon.

Let us write the simplified kinetic equations. The process is limited by the slowest stages—the synthesis of mRNA and enzymes. The rate at which mRNA increases depends hyperbolically on the amount of product P_1 activating the repressor, that is, on the amount of the enzyme that determines the synthesis of P. If we denote by x_1 the concentration of mRNA produced by the first operon, by x_2 the concentration of mRNA for the second operon, and by y_1 and y_2 the concentrations of the corresponding enzymes, then we obtain for mRNA's

$$\frac{dx_1}{dt} = \frac{A}{B + y_2} - kx_1$$
$$\frac{dx_2}{dt} = \frac{A}{B + y_1} - kx_2 \tag{91}$$

The terms $-kx$ describe the decay of mRNA. The rates of synthesis of mRNA are

$$\frac{dy_1}{dt} = ax_1 - by_1$$
$$\frac{dy_2}{dt} = ax_2 - by_2 \tag{92}$$

because the synthesis of enzymes is a template synthesis on mRNA.

We look again for the stationary solutions. In the stationary state, the time derivatives are equal to zero, and we get

$$k\frac{b}{a}y_1 = \frac{A}{B + y_2}$$
$$k\frac{b}{a}y_2 = \frac{A}{B + y_1} \tag{93}$$

The curves $y_2(y_1)$ corresponding to these equations are shown in Fig. 41. They intersect at only one point. Hence there is no switching in this case.

However, if blocking the gene operator requires the cooperative action of a repressor, that is, the simultaneous binding of several molecules by an operator, the situation changes. Let us assume

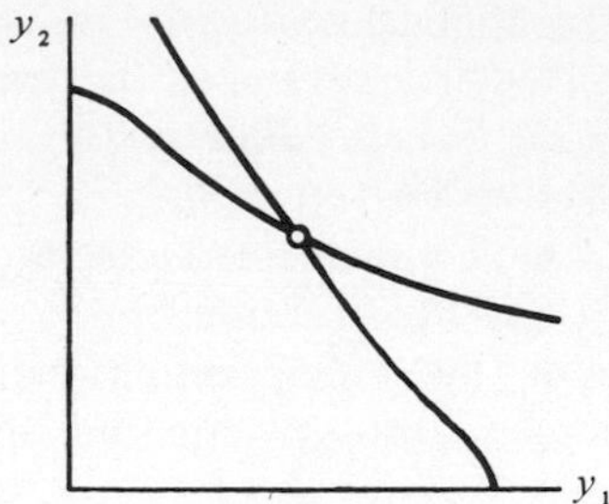

Fig. 41 Phase portrait of system (93).

that for repression, two molecules of repressor are necessary. Then, instead of Eqs. (91), we must write

$$\frac{dx_1}{dt} = \frac{A}{B + y_2^2} - kx_1$$
$$\frac{dx_2}{dt} = \frac{A}{B + y_1^2} - kx_2 \tag{94}$$

The equations for y_1, y_2 are again Eqs. (92). The stationary curves are

$$k\frac{b}{a}y_1 = \frac{A}{B + y_2^2}$$
$$k\frac{b}{a}y_2 = \frac{A}{B + y_1^2} \tag{95}$$

The phase portrait is different in this case (see Fig. 42). Curves (95) have three intersection points. The central point 1 is unstable; a small change of y_1 or y_2 transmits the system to the stable points 2 or 3. Hence the system possesses trigger properties; it can be switched

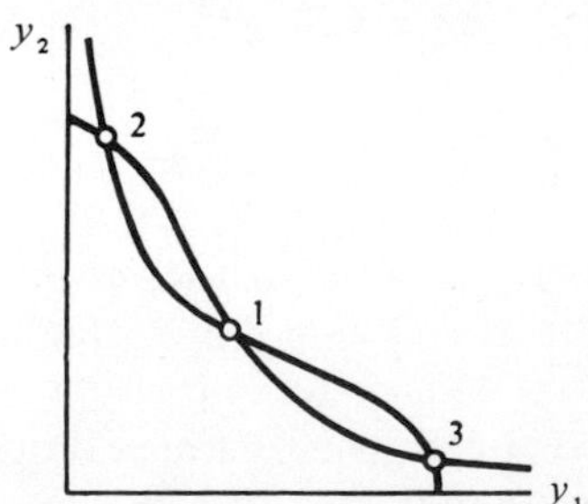

Fig. 42 Phase portrait of system (95).

from the state of preferential synthesis of protein E_1 to the stationary state corresponding to synthesis of protein E_2.

This is a rather simplified model of a trigger system. Very general reasoning leads to the conclusion that in a developing biological system there must be a multitude of stationary states, both stable and unstable. Coming from an unstable state, the system chooses one of the stable states; trigger switching occurs. Such a choice, determined by regulatory or fluctuant phenomena, means the creation of new information.

Of course, the model of the operon is too simplified to describe the behavior of a developing multicellular system. The problems of the physicomathematical modeling of cell differentiation and morphogenesis and of ontogenesis as a whole are not yet solved. However, the simplified description helps us understand some principal features of such systems.

Modeling has been successfully applied to solutions of a series of important biological problems, including enzymatic activity, biosynthetic processes, processes of development, and appearance of immunity. The work in the field of nonlinear nonequilibrium thermodynamics, which, as we have said, reduces to kinetics, belongs also to physicomathematical modeling, in particular to the modeling of autocatalytic processes. In all biophysical models, we meet with nonlinear differential equations.

Modeling explains such things as the processes of ordering in open dissipative systems far from equilibrium and the origin of the oscillatory regimes. Modeling allows us to select the parameters responsible for the behavior of the system and to predict the changes of this behavior that will result from definite changes of these parameters. Hence, using the physicomathematical model, experiments that support or refute the model can be performed. If the model is confirmed, we possess already the theory of the phenomenon.

Mathematical modeling in the field of population dynamics of micro- and macroorganisms has given already very interesting results with valuable applications in such areas as the establishment of optimal conditions for microbiological synthesis and of the scientific foundations of fishery. Scientific ecology is based on mathematical modeling (see [27, 28]).

The method of nonlinear differential equations considers the variables as changing continuously. Let them be, for instance, the numbers of individuals in the predator–prey model. This is a deterministic, causal description. In reality, the described systems has a discrete, statistical character. The numbers of individuals or molecules do not change continuously, and of course they are subject to random changes (fluctuations), which are especially noticeable if the number of objects is small, and hence, the values of the variables are small too. In the probabilistic description (stochastic models), the probabilities of single changes of the system must be taken into account. Thus, in the "predator–prey" model the probabilities of the birth and death of one hare and one lynx must be taken into account. Similarly in the stochastic description of enzymatic reactions, the probability of the number of molecules of the substrate or product changing by unity—the "birth" or "death" of a molecule—is accounted for. The deterministic description, with the help of differential equations, is valid if the number of the objects is sufficiently great; this description is an averaged one. Rigorous criteria for transferring from the probabilistic to the deterministic model can be formulated.

In the last years, a new trend has arisen in studies of the mathematical models of biological processes. Schlögl showed that in many cases, the behavior of a nonlinear system is similar to phase transitions in the physics of nonliving nature.

We spoke earlier about phase transition of the first kind—melting (Chapter 6). In such transitions, the fundamental thermodynamical quantities—enthalpy, volume, and entropy—break down. The properties of the real gas, which is able to transform into liquid, are described by the van der Waals equation

$$\left(p + \frac{a}{V^2}\right)(V - b) = RT \tag{96}$$

where p is pressure, V volume, T absolute temperature, and a, b, R are constants. This equation, in contrast with the Clapeyron equation for the ideal gas

$$pV = RT \tag{97}$$

takes into account the mutual attraction of molecules (with a/V^2) and their mutual repulsion (with b). The $p(V)$ curves for various temperatures—the isotherms corresponding to Eq. (96)—are shown in Fig. 43. At temperatures lower than $T = T_{cr}$, the curves are rather peculiar; they possess maxima and minima. In reality, during the gradual increase of the pressure, the state of gas at $T < T_{cr}$ will not change along the curve $ABCDEFG$. At point B the gas will compress, that is, the pressure will remain constant (straight line BDF)

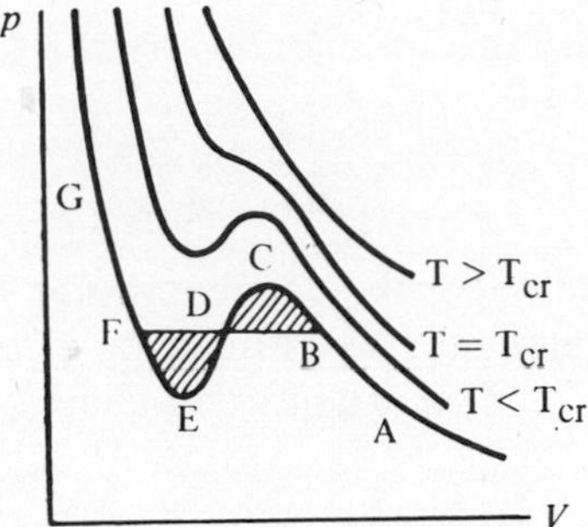

Fig. 43 Van der Waals isotherms.

until the gas transforms totally into liquid, that is, until the phase transition ends.

The straight line *BF* can be found from Maxwell's condition: the equality of the areas *BDC* and *DEF*. At critical temperature T_{cr}, the whole segment *BCDEF* is transformed into a point, and at $T > T_{cr}$ the behavior of the real gas is like that of the ideal one and its isotherm lacks any singularities. At the curve's point of inflection, the first and second derivatives of p by V are equal to zero:

$$\left(\frac{\partial p}{\partial V}\right)_T = -\frac{RT}{(V-b)^2} + \frac{2a}{V^3} = 0$$
$$\left(\frac{\partial^2 p}{\partial V^2}\right)_T = \frac{2RT}{(V-b)^3} - \frac{6a}{V^4} = 0 \tag{98}$$

From Eqs. (96)–(98), the critical values of temperature, pressure, and volume can be derived:

$$T_{cr} = \frac{8}{27}\frac{a}{Rb},$$
$$p_{cr} = \frac{1}{27}\frac{a}{b^2}, \tag{99}$$
$$V_{cr} = 3b$$

Let us now consider the chemical reactions according to Schlögl,

$$A + 2X \underset{k_{-1}}{\overset{k_1}{\rightleftharpoons}} 3X$$
$$B + X \underset{k_{-2}}{\overset{k_2}{\rightleftharpoons}} C$$

The first reaction is autocatalytic; the amount of substance X increases under the action of X on A. Here k_1, k_{-1}, k_2, k_{-2} are the rate constants. The rates of reactions from left to right are

$$\begin{aligned} v_1 &= k_1AX^2 - k_{-1}X^3, \\ v_2 &= k_2BX - k_{-2}C, \end{aligned} \tag{100}$$

where A, B, C, and X are the concentrations of the corresponding substances. For simplicity, let us take $k_{-1} = 1$, $k_1A = 3$, and let us denote k_2B as β, $k_{-2}C$ as γ. The rate of change of the concentration X is equal to

$$\begin{aligned} \frac{dX}{dt} &= v_1 - v_2 \\ &= -X^3 + 3X^2 - \beta X + \gamma \end{aligned} \tag{101}$$

Under stationary conditions, $v_1 = v_2$ and expression (101) is equal to zero. Hence

$$\gamma = X^3 - 3X^2 + \beta X \tag{102}$$

The curves $\gamma(X)$ representing Eq. (102) are shown in Fig. 44, which is very similar to Fig. 42. The equation

$$\frac{dX}{dt} = 0$$

has three roots, which coincide at the critical value $\beta = \beta_{cr}$. Critical values of variable X and of parameters γ and β are

$$\begin{aligned} X_{cr} &= 1, \\ \gamma_{cr} &= 1, \\ \beta_{cr} &= 3 \end{aligned} \tag{103}$$

Three different real, positive roots $X_2 > X_3 > X_1$ are possible only at $\beta < \beta_{cr}$. The solutions X_1, X_2 are stable, and the unstable root X_3 is

Fig. 44 The curves $\gamma(X)$ [Eq. (102)].

located at the decreasing branch of $\gamma(X)$. Comparison of Figs. 42 and 43 shows that the concentration X plays the role of density V^{-1}, the value γ corresponds to pressure p, and the value β corresponds to RT.

In this autocatalytic system, at $\beta < 3$ a transition between the two stable stationary states X_1 and X_2 similar to the liquid–gas phase transition of the first kind occurs. This is important in biophysics, which shows that autocatalytic chemical reactions determine the ordering in biological development, particularly of differentiation and morphogenesis. For other autocatalytic processes, the analogs of phase transitions of the second kind such as the ferromagnetic–paramagnetic transitions, can be shown.

There are grounds for thinking that biological development—both ontogenetic and phylogenetic—occurs like some phase transitions. It has been shown with the help of mathematical models that the formation of a new species in an evolutionary population is like a phase transition [19].

The studies of nonequilibrium phase transitions—the formation of well organized structures out of chaotic ones—are a new and very important field of natural science, which is called synergetics. This is a broad field of physics, chemistry, and biology that includes such phenomena as biological evolution and cooperative ordering in lasers [19, 31].

Now we shall consider the problems of biological development.

CHAPTER 11

Problems of Development

The most important general problems of life are the problems of development. The decisive stage in the construction of scientific biology was Darwin's proposal of the theory of evolution. This theory had no relation to physics. Only now is the situation beginning to change, and we are approaching an understanding of the physical sense of phylogenesis and ontogenesis.

The problems of development are not alien to physics. Physics met with them in the studies of the solar system and of the universe as a whole. Astrophysics, like biophysics, is the physics of historic, developing objects. In their studies we meet with the rise of order as the result of transition of an open system from an unstable into a relatively stable state far from equilibrium. Stars, galaxies, and the universe as a whole are nonequilibrium systems. Ultimately, life is determined by the nonequilibrium state of the sun. Life cannot exist without solar radiation.

Scientific biology postulates the abiogenic origin of life, as suggested by Oparin in 1924. He assumed that the primary atmosphere of Earth was reductive—it did not contain free oxygen (O_2); it contained H_2, CH_4, H_2O, NH_3, and CO_2. It has been shown experimentally that the electrical discharge through such a mixture of gases or its irradiation by ultraviolet light produces complicated organic substances, including amino acids and nucleotides. Oxygen appeared in the atmosphere later as the result of photosynthesis in plants. Newest data show, however, that oxygen could be formed in big amounts in the atmosphere by the photodissociation of water. It is not clear yet how complex organic substances could be formed in the presence of O_2. This, however, does not contradict the abiogenic origin of life [19].

Evidently, monomeric molecules were polymerized. The polymeric chains of proteins and nucleic acids formed were the first ingredients of future cells.

The fundamental problem of the theory of the origin of life is the rise of ordered informational macromolecules, the rise of texts from a random mixture of monomers, the formation of order from chaos. This problem seemed to be insoluble for many outstanding physicists. Wigner came to the conclusion that life is incompatible with quantum mechanics [32]. He was mistaken because he did not take into account the ability of biopolymers (nucleic acids) to play the role of biosynthetic templates.

Order can arise from chaos as the result of random processes if the system contains reproducible and destructible units. Let us consider the following game [33]: a box contains N balls of different colors. For simplicity, let $N = 7$—we have a red, an orange, a yellow, a green, a sky-blue, a blue, and a violet ball. Besides that, we have an unlimited supply of the balls of all seven colors in a bag. We take at random one ball from the box and put it aside. This ball "died." We make the same operation once more, but now the ball does not "die" but is "reproduced"—we take a ball of the same color from the bag and put both balls back in the box. We alternate further "death" and "reproduction." It is easy to see that after some number of these events, the box will contain seven balls of one color—order will arise from disorder. Of course, this game does not model evolution as there is no selection, no conditions for preferential reproduction of the balls of definite color. The system chooses the color of remaining balls at random. However, order arises from chaos.

The evolutionary system in which the informational macromolecules can be formed must be open, far from equilibrium, and supplied with energy. The system must possess the ability of transition from unstable states into relatively stable ones. The corresponding physicomathematical model has been proposed and investigated by Eigen [19, 34].

Let us imagine a box with semipermeable walls. Monomers but no polymers can transfer through them. In the box, the monomers polymerize and the polymeric chains are destructed at random. The chains have the ability to replicate, acting as template catalyzers. The replication can be partly erroneous; mutations occur. The system is a nonequilibrium one, and the monomers possess an excess of chemical energy such as ATP.

The rates of copying, or reproduction, are different for various chains. Evidently, those chains for which the rate of replication will be less than the rate of decay into monomers will "die out." On the contrary, the chains whose reproduction occurs faster than decay, will "survive."

However, this process does not yet model natural selection. Only if we introduce in our open systems (Eigen's box) some constraints providing the steady organization, that is, the constancy of the concentration of monomeric units both in free monomers and in the polymerized chains, will selection and evolution occur. Every kind of chains differing by the sequence of monomers can be characterized by its own rate of reproduction. It is important that the mistakes of copying—the mutations—can decrease or increase this rate.

The chains possess definite selective value expressed by the combination of kinetic constants characterizing the exceeding rate of replication and taking mutations into account. The solution of kinetic equations—the mathematical analysis of the model—shows that after some lapse of time only those chains that possess the maximal selective value will remain in the system. They will be accumulated because of the dying out of all other chains. The presence of mutations is necessary for the evolution. If new chains of the exceeding selective value will arise as the result of mutations, the process will be shifted toward the formation of these chains.

Eigen showed that the "natural selection" of such a kind and evolution can proceed in a stable way in the systems known as hypercycles which contain nucleic acids and enzymes coded by them, catalyzing the replication of the nucleic acids. The code relations between nucleic acids and proteins are necessary at a very early stage of prebiological evolution.

The scheme of a hypercycle according to Eigen is shown in Fig. 45. Here I_i are the carriers of information, that is, complementary threads of RNA. Every small cycle denotes the self-instructing properties of a collective I_i containing two complementary chains. Such collectives code the enzymes E_4, which in their turn catalyze the formation of the new collectives. The hypercycle as a whole is closed, which means that there exists an enzyme E_4 that helps the formation of I_1. Except for this, the side branches of biochemical reactions which do not participate in selection occur. Selection occurs between the hypercycles. This model is described by nonlinear

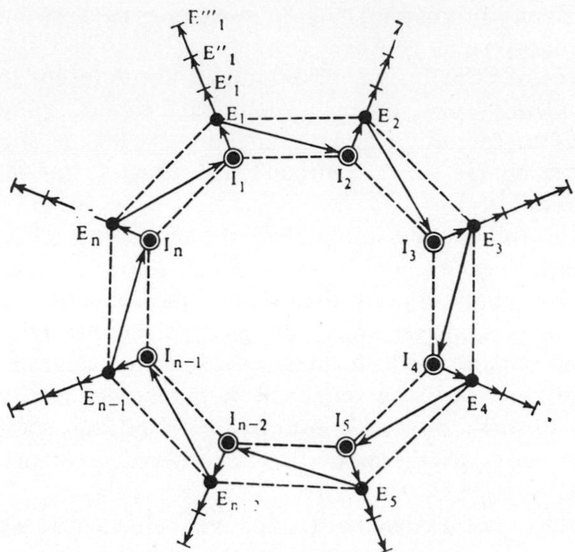

Fig. 45 Scheme of a hypercycle according to Eigen.

differential equations, but it can be investigated also at the basis of probabilistic relations. The equivalence of both approaches has been proved by Eigen.

This model theory could be compared with experiments of Spiegelman, who investigated the $Q\beta$-phage. The $Q\beta$-phage, which is infectious for some bacterial cells, synthesizes in them the enzyme $Q\beta$-replicase. This enzyme catalyzes the reproduction of the phage, that is, the template replication of its RNA. The enzyme $Q\beta$-replicase is quite specific: it recognizes only the $Q\beta$-RNA but no other RNA.

Spiegelman studied "the evolution in a test-tube." Replicase and activated monomers were put into a vessel, where a minor quantity of $Q\beta$-RNA served as a template. The template replicative synthesis of the same RNA occurred. A small fraction of the synthesized RNA was transmitted as initiator into the next test-tube, which contained monomers and replicase, etc. The time used for the synthesis is every next probe (incubation time) decreased steadily. Eighty transfers were performed.

Evidently here is observed the selection of those RNA chains which possess the highest rate of reproduction. At the end, the molecules of RNA that have lost 85% of their initial links, but preserved the ability to interact with replicase, were obtained. These molecules have the highest selective value according to Eigen. The calculations agree with these experiments.

The theory of Eigen consists in the construction of a physicomathematical model of the prebiological evolution of macromolecules. At the same time, this theory is directly connected with nonequilibrium thermodynamics in the region which is far from equilibrium. In Fig. 46, the scheme of dependence of the entropy of the system on time is shown, the total flows of monomeric units being constant. The formation of a mutated chain with selective advantage corresponds to the negative entropy fluctuation that produces nonstability. The primary selected chains become destructed, and the number of mutated chains increases toward dominating level. As new and old chains possess equal energy, the slopes of the straight lines $S(t)$ representing the entropy production in the steady states, that is, the dissipation function σ are also equal. The constant difference of the entropy curves in the steady states reflect the increase of order expressed by the growth of the system organization.

Of course the theory of Eigen does not pretend that the prebiological evolution was performed on Earth just in the described way. The theory is only a model, showing the principal possibility of such evolution based on the well established principles of physics and chemistry. The most important conclusion is the sufficiency of these principles for explanation of the prebiological Darwinian evolution, and, hence, of the biological evolution, too. We have to introduce some new physical notions as the selective value, but there is no need of revision of the general principles of physics. Further development of these ideas allowed construction of the models of biological evolution [19, 23, 28].

The physical theory shows that the order can arise from chaos because of the template synthesis, that informational macromolecules can be formed in a random mixture of monomers.

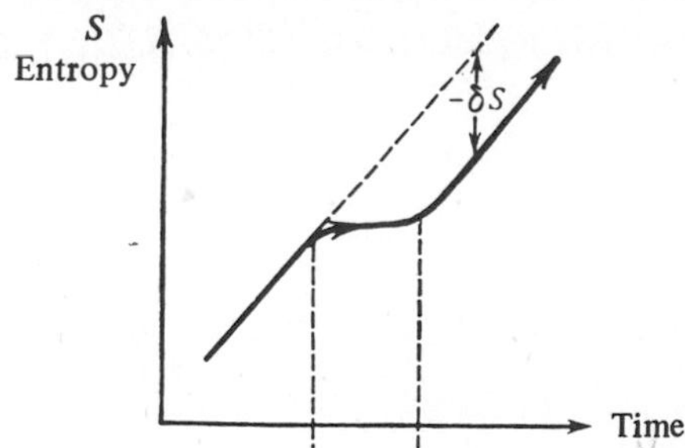

Fig. 46 Dependence of entropy of an evolutionary system on time.

Let us consider another simple example of ordering which has also a direct relationship with evolution. As it was told already in Chapter 6, the amino acids contained in all proteins of living organisms possess the *L* (left) configuration. How could selection occur between right and left molecules with equal chemical properties at the stage of prebiological evolution?

Let x_D and x_L be the numbers of molecules of the primary biopolymers formed by right and left, D- and L-monomers m_D and m_L. The rates of formation of x_D from m_D and of x_L from m_L are equal; the rates of decay are equal, too. The kinetic equations describing the development of the system have the form

$$\frac{dx_L}{dt} = ax_L w_L - bx_L \qquad \frac{dx_D}{dt} = ax_D w_D - bx_D \tag{104}$$

where a is the polymerization constant, b is the rate constant of decay, and w_L and w_D are the probabilities of meeting of templates x_L and x_D with monomers m_L and m_D correspondingly. These probabilities are

$$w_L = \frac{m_L}{m_L + m_D} \qquad w_D = \frac{m_D}{m_L + m_D} \tag{105}$$

At every value of m_L and m_D,

$$x_L x_D = x_L(0)x_D(0)e^{(a-2b)t} \tag{106}$$

where $x_L(0)$ and $x_D(0)$ are the values of x_L and x_D at the initial moment ($t = 0$). The system is stationary if $a = 2b$. The condition of stationarity corresponds to the equivalent mixture of monomers, $w_D = w_L = 0.5$, that is, $m_D = m_L$. However, this stationary state is unstable. If a random fluctuation occurs, $m_D \neq m_L$ and ($\alpha > 0$)

$$w_L = 0.5 + \alpha, \qquad w_D = 0.5 - \alpha \tag{107}$$

Then the solutions of equations (104) have the form

$$x_L = x_L(0)e^{(a/2-b)t}e^{a\alpha t} \qquad x_D = x_D(0)e^{(a/2-b)t}e^{-a\alpha t} \tag{108}$$

and with the lapse of time, the population x_L becomes dominating as

$$\frac{x_L}{x_D} = \frac{x_L(0)}{x_D(0)} e^{2a\alpha t} \tag{109}$$

We can think that the selection of a definite chirality of amino acids and nucleotides occurred because of the growth of the random fluctuative declination from the stationary state which happened to be unstable. It is clear that the choice of the "sign" of the monomer means the creation of new information (equal to one bit per link), and the decrease of entropy.

Everybody who thinks about biological evolution meets with the problem of time. If life originated in an abiogenic way and its evolution followed Darwin's theory, was the time sufficient for the creation of the existing multitude of biological species? According to contemporary data, the universe has existed for $\sim 2 \times 10^{10}$ years, and Earth for $\sim 5 \times 10^9$ years; the first unicellular organisms were formed $\sim 4 \times 10^9$ years ago, and the first multicellular organisms $\sim 10^9$ years ago.

The contemporary model theory answers this question in a positive way: there was sufficient time. The basic physicochemical principle of evolution is that the biological (genetic) information once obtained is not lost. At every stage of development, there is no random choice of all possible mutations, as the main part of mutations does not participate in selection, which proceeds only between those mutations consistent with the conditions of existence of the already living organisms. Therefore the evolution becomes "channelized" and accelerated. There is some similarity between evolution and the game of chess (with that difference that there is no "chess-player," no Supreme Being playing this game in biology). At the initial position, every partner can make 20 different moves, but everybody knowing the play a little chooses between 5 and 6 moves. Later the number of possible moves increases till 40 and more but simultaneously the number of reasonable moves decreases. At the final stage, at the Endspiel the number of possible moves is small and the smaller becomes the number of moves which are left for consideration. The chess-player never considers all possible moves, throwing away their main fraction. After every move a new situation occurs at the chessboard. In a similar way each new level of evolutionary development means not only the change of the evolving population but also the change of the conditions of the environment. All interacting species participate in evolution simultaneously (however with very differing rates). This produces the "channelization," the "sharpening" of the evolutionary process. The ideas of the contemporary theory of games are very useful for the construction of the theory of evolution [32].

The biological developmental system of immunity is comparatively well studied. The work of an immune system is that the organism produces specific reactive cells (cellular immune response), and specific proteins-antibodies (AB) (humoral immune response) in response to the introduction of an alien genetically biopolymeric material-antigen (AG). Cells and antibodies interact with AG. As the result of this interaction the alien material, for example the pathogenic microorganisms, can be inactivated or destructed. The contemporary notions of immunity are based on the clonal-selective theory of Australian biologist F. Burnet.

In the organism of a vertebrate a multitude of different lymphocytes is produced susceptible practically to any AG including those which will never be met by the organism in conditions of its biological existence. This is due to the presence of specific receptors at the membranes of lymphocytes. These receptors bind definite antigens. AG act as selection factors stimulating the development of the clones of immunologically active cells containing the lymphocytes with high affinity to the given AG. Antibodies are produced by lymphocytes which have experienced a series of transformations stimulated by AG. The so-called B-lymphocytes do not divide but they obtain the ability for division, for proliferation only after the blast-transformation, i.e. only after the transformation into the so-called blasts under the influence of AG. A fraction of blasts initiate the clones of plasmatic cells which produce antibodies. These cells do not divide further and exist during some tens of hours.

B-lymphocytes stimulated by AG are transformed also into the clone of the cells of immune memory. If the organism interacts with AG which influenced the organism earlier usually its secondary immune response is stronger and occurs faster. This is the phenomenon of immune memory. It is connected with the increase of the number of cells able to respond to the repeated antigenic stimulus in a way analogous to the primary B-lymphocytes.

A physicomathematical model of the humoral immunity has been constructed [19, 35]. The model describes the temporal changes of the numbers of B-lymphocytes, antigens, and antibodies with the help of a system of nonlinear differential equations. The reproductive ability of antigen is taken into account. The equations are similar to the equations of Volterra or to the equations of Lotka, describing the kinetics of autocatalytic chemical reactions. However it was necessary to take into account directly the times of delay—the rate of AB production is proportional to the existing number of plasmatic cells which is determined by the number of B-lymphocytes, stimulated earlier at the moment of time which was away from the considered one by the time of delay. The similar situation exists for the memory cells. The investigation of the model shows that depending on the parameters such as the time of delay various situations can occur during the infectious disease. First, the system may tend toward constant quantity of AG without the development of the disease. This is the state of the infection carrier. Second, the periodic change of the quantity of AG is possible—the periodic proceeding of the disease. Third, going through the maximum the quantity of AG may tend toward zero—it is the recovery. And, fourth, beginning at some moment the quantity of AG can grow without limit. This is the development of infection and destruction of the patient.

Thus, physicomathematical study allows to approach some practical problems of medicine to find the optimal tactics of healing. It is shown for instance, that the introduction of immune vaccines produces the highest effect when the maximal amount of AB is already formed in the organism. The earlier application of vaccines and also of antibiotics weakens the immune response and, hence, increases the probability of relapse.

The model shows that in the case of weak chronic infections one of the methods of treatment can be the intentional transfer of the disease into a sharper form. Thus the immune response can be activated and the probability of the total elimination of AG can be increased.

CHAPTER 12

Biological Development and Information Theory

The biological theory of evolution can be translated into the language of information theory. This was done by Schmalhausen [36], with very instructive results. Using the canonical theory of information, which considers only the amount of information, Schmalhausen uncovered the direct and feedback connections that determine the evolutionary process, and hence made the picture more clear. However, Schmalhausen emphasized that the usual theory of information is quite insufficient for biology. The usual theory considers only the amount of information contained in some message irrespective of its sense. We obtain one bit of information in the "yes" or "no" answer to a question, that is, in the solution of the dual alternative. Thus, we obtain one bit of information by throwing a coin or by answering the question of whether the second law of thermodynamics is applicable to living systems—if we do not know anything about this problem.

Of course, we get one bit only if both answers are of equal probability for us, that is, if we do not possess any preliminary knowledge about the problem. The total separation from the contents of the message is an advantage of information theory. This theory is used in particular for calculating the delivery capacity of communication channels. Clearly, the theory would be totally useless if it were to take into account the contents of the telegrams in calculating the number of telegrams of definite length that can be delivered by a given line.

Correspondingly, the usual theory of information does not consider the reception of information. It is assumed only that the receiver can distinguish one letter from another; he knows the difference between "yes" and "no" or between two sides of a coin. His abilities are very restricted.

Evidently, such a theory of information cannot be very useful for biology. For instance, investigating the informational aspects of the genetic message carried by the DNA text, we find that for biology what is important is the function of DNA—programming the protein synthesis—and not the amount of information in DNA that can be easily calculated (Chapter 9). Not the quantity but the quality of information is of interest here; the contents or value of information in a message is applied in a concrete biological process.

The value of information is determined by events caused by reception of the message; hence it can be evaluated only in terms of the consequences of reception. Reception means the alteration of the receiving system: if the system does not change under the action of the message, then there is no reception at all. Evidently the reception of information is an irreversible process occurring in a nonequilibrium system characterized by the existence of unstable states. The reception of information transfers the system from the unstable state into a relatively stable one.

Reception is a process that occurs at various levels. The value of information depends on the level of reception—a given message can possess high value for one receiver and zero value for another one. Hence it is impossible to obtain a general definition of the value of information such as the definition of its amount. However, we can connect the value of information with its redundancy.

At a given level, only nonredundant information, that is, information that is as yet unknown by the receiver and that can be perceived, has any value. What is the meaning of redundancy? Let us explain this concept with the help of linguistics. If only the number N of different letters in a language is known, then the amount of information per letter is equal to

$$I_1 = \log_2 N \tag{110}$$

For Russian, $N = 32$ and $I_1 = 5$ bits. This is the first level of reception. At the next level, the elementary structure of the language—the probabilities of the appearance of different letters p_i—is known (for example, in English the letter y is much rarer than the letter a). The amount of information per letter can be calculated by Shannon's formula

$$I_2 = -\sum_{i=1}^{N} p_i \log_2 p_i \tag{111}$$

where the probabilities p_i are normalized, that is, their sum is equal to unity

$$\sum_{i=1}^{N} p_i = 1 \tag{112}$$

It is easy to show that $I_2 < I_1$, that is, the amount of information per letter diminishes when there is preliminary information about the frequency of each letter's appearance. At this level, the message contains redundant information. Redundancy is given by

$$R_2 = 1 - \frac{I_2}{I_1} \tag{113}$$

Redundancy R_2 shows the difference between unity and the ratio of the information I_2 perceived by the system to the arriving information I_1 [37].

At the next level, the pairwise correlations between letters are taken into account (thus, in Russian the vowel follows the consonant more frequently than another vowel). Then the triple correlations can be taken into account. Redundancy

$$R_j = 1 - \frac{I_j}{I_1} \tag{114}$$

increases in the sequence of levels. Thus, for the English language,

I_1	I_2	I_3	I_4	⋯	I_6	⋯	I_9
4.76	4.03	3.32	3.1	⋯	2.1	⋯	1.9 bits

and the redundancies are

R_1	R_2	R_3	R_4	⋯	R_6	⋯	R_9
0	0.15	0.3	0.35	⋯	0.56	⋯	0.60

This means that at the ninth level, 60% of the letters contained in a message are redundant. The remaining 40% are sufficient for understanding the message. Let us remember how the text of a letter found in a bottle in Jules Verne's *The Children of Captain Grant* was deciphered. Most of the letters had been washed out by water, but the remaining letters were sufficient for the nearly total restoration of the text.

The increase of the reception level increases the redundancy of information and, hence, the value—the irreplaceability—of the remaining nonredundant elements of the message. We can now formulate a definition of the value of information [38].

The message contains n_1 letters and an amount of information n_1I_1. At the next level, the amount of nonredundant information is smaller—n_1I_2. We can replace the decrease of the amount of information per letter by the decrease of the number of letters in the message. In other words, we assume that

$$n_1I_2 = n_2I_1 \tag{115}$$

The effective number of letters decreased

$$\frac{I_1}{I_2} = \frac{1}{1 - R_2}$$

times, and the information per one letter increased the same number of times. We define the relative value of information in the same way. Thus the relative values at subsequent levels of reception are

$$\frac{I_1}{I_2}, \frac{I_1}{I_3}, \ldots, \frac{I_1}{I_j}$$

For the English language, these numbers are

$$1, 1.18, 1.43, 1.54, \ldots 2.28, \ldots 2.50$$

The increase of the level corresponds to the increase of the value—or irreplaceability—of the nonredundant element of a message.

Let us consider a corresponding biological example. The amount of information in a DNA chain containing n links can be defined as

$$\begin{aligned} I_1 &= n \log_2 N \\ &\equiv n \log_2 4 \\ &= 2n \text{ bits} \end{aligned} \tag{116}$$

This information is valuable for protein synthesis if the corresponding gene is not repressed. Evidently the value is directly connected with the instability of the system in which the protein is synthesized. If a DNA chain is introduced into the system, it will produce a definite protein chain. The amount of information in the protein chain is smaller than in DNA:

$$\begin{aligned} I_2 &= \frac{n}{3} \log_2 N' \\ &\equiv \frac{n}{3} \log_2 20 \\ &= 1.44\, n \text{ bits} \end{aligned} \tag{117}$$

The decrease of the amount of information is due to the degeneracy of the code. Redundancy is

$$R_2 = 1 - \frac{I_2}{I_1} = 0.28 \tag{118}$$

and the ratio of the values of I_2 and I_1 is 1.39 : 1. At the next level, we shall take into account the substitutions of amino acid residues without pronounced changes of the protein properties. If the residues are similar, their hydrophobicities do not differ much. Such replacements are actually possible. Let us assume that there are five mutually replaceable amino acids. We get

$$I_3 = \frac{n}{3}\log_2 16 = 1.33\,n \text{ bits} \tag{119}$$

Redundancy at this level is equal to

$$R_3 = 1 - \frac{I_3}{I_1} = 0.33 \tag{120}$$

and the ratios of values of I_3, I_2, I_1 are 1.50 : 1.39 : 1.00. Taking into account the replaceabilities of some proteins, we get further increase of the value of information. The value of information is discussed in the literature [19, 38–41].

We must distinguish between the reception of information entering the system, and the creation of new information in a system. Except for mutations, no new information is created in Eigen's model, which considers the selective value; instead, preexisting information or value is revealed. By contrast, in the selection of the chiral links, new information is created in the system as the result of a random declination from the unstable stationary state.

According to Quastler [42], the creation of new information is the memorizing of accidental choice. What does this mean? Quastler gives an example: a man leaves his luggage in an automatic cloakroom. He chooses some arbitrary numerical code and memorizes it. Only by knowing this code can one open the cloakroom. Information has been created.

In biology, new information is created in the origination of every new individuum as the result of sexual reproduction. An unprogrammed recombination of genes appears. Sexual reproduction is the cause of very broad variability that gives unlimited material for evolution.

New information is produced by the creative activity of man. The great Russian poet Alexander Blok wrote: "A poet is the child of harmony, and he possesses some role in the world's culture. He is charged with three tasks: first, to liberate the sounds from their native elements, which lack any beginning; second, to arrange these sounds into harmony, to give them a form; third, to introduce this harmony into the external world" [43].

If we translate these poetic words into the dry language of information theory, it becomes clear that the first and second tasks of the poet are the creation of new information.

A biological system is characterized by pronounced hierarchy of its levels of information reception. In ontogenic development, the informative messages become specialized and irreplaceable, and hence information becomes valuable. Simultaneously, the amount of information increases at higher levels of organization, that is, along with the initial genetic information new information is created, coded not only by the sequence of nucleotides themselves but also by the organization of the cellular structures and by the morphology of the organism.

Fascinating experiments have been performed in developmental biology. For example, the properties of different sites of a newt embryo have been established. It is known that at an early stage of embryonic development, a definite site takes part in the formation of the eye. This site can be called presumptive eye. If it is transplanted into an embryo at a higher stage of development, the fate of the presumptive eye will depend on the site of transplantation. In the region of the host's head it forms a brain or an eye; transplanted into other parts of the embryo it forms other organs that would appear in these parts in the course of normal development. However, if the site is taken from the later embryo it forms only an eye wherever it is transplanted, even at the tail or paw. The presumptive eye becomes a determined one.

Thus the irreplaceability and the value of information of a given structure increases in the course of biological development. The same is shown by the similarity of the early embryos of fish, amphibians, birds, and mammals, and their increasing divergence and specialization during further development.

Similar processes occur in biological evolution. The divergence of species according to Darwin, that is, their ecological and sexual incompatibility, means the growth of irreplaceability, and hence of the value of information. We came to the conclusion that the value increases in both ontogenetic and phylogenetic development.

These concepts about the value of information can be applied to every kind of information, including artistic information. Reception of artistic information is always connected with a definite level of preliminary training. I cannot read a poem if I do not know the language in which it is written. However, this is not sufficient. There must be instability, in this case, a goal—the aspiration to read this poem [38, 44].

We evaluate information according to its irreplaceability, and we define the value of an element of a message by the consequences of its substitution. The stronger are the changes produced in the receptive system by the substitution of the element, the higher is the element's value. In this sense, the value of a word in an artistic text is much higher than in a scientific one. The same scientific thesis can be expressed by different words, but the substitution of only one word in a good poem changes its total informational structure. Let us consider the genetic code from this point of view [19, 45].

The substitution of one letter in the codon xyz (Chapter 7) means a point mutation. In many cases, such a substitution changes the coded amino acid. This change strongly influences the properties of the protein if the change of hydrophobicity is great. Correspondingly, the value of the codon is higher the greater is the average change of hydrophobicity of amino acid due to all possible substitutions of the letters x,y,z in the codon. This change can be expressed by values characterizing hydrophobicity, that is, in calories per mole. The hydrophobicities of amino acids were listed in Table I (Chapter 6). Using these data and the genetic code in Table II (Chapter 7), we obtain conventional values, which are represented in Table II.

We see that the values of the degenerate codons responsible for one amino acid differ. Thus the codons GGA, GGC, GGG, and GGU responsible for Gly have the values 1.7, 1.4, 2.5, and 1.4. The most valuable codon is UGG, responsible for Trp: mutations of this codon produce especially great changes of hydrophobicity, and are therefore very dangerous.

Three codons—UAA, UAG, UGA—are terminal, that is, responsible for breaking the protein chain. Therefore, mutations that produce these codons are especially dangerous. It can be shown that the substitutions A → G and G → A have the highest probabilities.

Thus the codon UGG is the most valuable. Two out of nine point mutations of this codon give the terminal codons, and both these mutations are the substitutions A → G:

$$\text{UGG} \rightarrow \text{UAG}$$

and

$$\text{UGG} \rightarrow \text{UGA}$$

Many primary structures of proteins, including those of homologous proteins of different species, such as mutant proteins, are known. For example, the hemoglobin texts of many vertebrates and a series of the sequences in mutant human hemoglobins have been established. Using such data, Bachinsky obtained the table of mutual replaceabilities of amino acids in proteins. On the basis of this table, a scale of values of amino acid residues can be established and arranged according to their irreplaceabilities. The rarer are substitutions for the residue, the higher is its value. Only the single substitutions in codons are taken into account. The data relating to degenerate codons are summarized and averaged. Conventional values are given in Table V. The most valuable are the residues Trp, Met, and Cys; the least valuable, Gly, Val, and Ala.

These data characterize amino acid residues and codons better than the hydrophobicities of amino acids (see [19, 45]).

Let us try to check the thesis about the growth of value in the course of evolution. Comparison of substitutions in the evolutionary tree of hemoglobins with the values established for amino acid residues does not give any reasonable results. The summary differences of values for human hemoglobin and hemoglobins of a series of vertebrates are positive or negative without any regularity. This is not surprising. Even the hemoglobins of related species differ by many residues, and the sum of conventional averaged characteristics evidently has no meaning for hemoglobin.

TABLE V

VALUES OF AMINO ACID RESIDUES CHARACTERIZING THE DEGREE OF THEIR IRREPLACEABILITY[a]

1. Trp	1.82	6. Phe	0.86	11. Glu	0.76	16. Leu	0.58
2. Met	1.25	7. Gln	0.86	12. Ile	0.65	17. Thr	0.56
3. Cys	1.12	8. Lys	0.81	13. Ser	0.64	18. Gly	0.56
4. Tyr	0.98	9. Asn	0.79	14. Pro	0.61	19. Val	0.54
5. His	0.94	10. Asp	0.77	15. Arg	0.60	20. Ala	0.52

[a] Conventional units.

In contrast, comparison of the amino acid composition of cytochromes *c*, which are very ancient and universal proteins, is rather instructive. The data are listed in Table VI, which shows the difference between the sum of values of residues in cytochrome *c* of various mammals and that of man, and the similar difference between cytochrome *c* of various birds and that of the penguin. The minus sign indicates a value less than that of man or penguin.

In a rough way, the sequences of the values of cytochromes *c* reproduce evolutionary sequences. The value grows in the course of phylogenesis.

We must discuss these data. Why is the value of the human cytochrome *c* the highest among mammals? The respiratory enzyme—cytochrome *c*—has no relationship to the development of the brain.

More valuable amino acid residues are more irreplaceable; therefore, they are more stable in the substitutions. The growth of the value of cytochrome *c* reflects a longer evolution, a greater number of mutational replacements of residues. Man had a longer path of evolution than other animals.

Kimura has show that at the molecular level, there is no natural selection that acts at the level of phenotypes. Mutations of nucleic acids and corresponding proteins are mainly neutral, and the evolutionary changes that occur in the primary structures of biopolymers

TABLE VI

DIFFERENCES OF THE SUMS OF VALUES OF AMINO ACID RESIDUES IN CYTOCHROMES *c*

Mammals		Birds	
Man	0.00	Penguin	0.00
Rhesus monkey	−0.10	Chicken	−0.05
Donkey	−0.34	Emu	−0.30
Horse	−0.43	Duck	−0.30
Pig	−0.58	Pigeon	−0.58
Rabbit	−0.66		
Whale	−0.88	Turtle[a]	−1.30
Kangaroo	−0.88		
Dog	−1.06		
Elephant	−1.22		
Bat	−1.24		

[a] Although the turtle is a reptile, it is useful to compare it with birds.

are the results of the random drift of genes. The main argument in favor of this neutralistic theory is the approximate constancy of the rate of protein evolution expressed by the number of amino acid substitutions per year (or million of years). This rate is different for different proteins: it is much higher for hemoglobin than for cytochrome *c*, and the smallest rate corresponds to histones. This means that functional constraints reduce the rate of molecular evolution (see [46]).

The neutralistic theory has been strongly criticized as "anti-Darwinian." However, this criticism is not convincing, and Kimura gave a proper answer to it [46]. In reality there is no contradiction between Kimurian and Darwinian evolution. We shall now try to understand the physical meaning of neutralism.

Genes code only the primary structure of proteins. Natural selection acts at the level of their phenotypic, physiological function. Were there no correlation between the primary structure of protein and its function, molecular biology would be senseless. Of course such a correlation exists—but is it unambiguous or not?

Actually, we should speak about two correlations: the correlation between the primary and spatial structure, and the correlation between the spatial structure of proteins and their biological function. It has been established that the first correlation is ambiguous and degenerate: various amino acid sequences correspond to the same spatial structure of the protein (this is especially clear in the case of globins). There are grounds for thinking that the second correlation is also ambiguous. Hence neutralism means the degeneracy of the primary structures of biopolymers [47].

The neutralistic theory must be developed further. Till now only the amino acidic composition of proteins has been taken into account. However, the protein molecule is a complex structure that consists, roughly speaking, of two subsystems: the active site with its nearest surroundings, and the remainder protein moiety. The first subsystem is subjected to much stronger constraints than the second one. Therefore, neutral mutations are much more probable in the second subsystem than in the first one. The active subsystem is mainly Darwinian, the passive one mainly Kimurian. The relative role of the two subsystems is different for different proteins. Hemoglobin is more Kimurian than cytochrome *c*, and in histones the whole protein molecule can be considered as one active system. This is the explanation of the different behaviors of hemoglobin and cytochrome *c* from the point of view of the value of information.

The amount of information also increases in the course of an organism's biological development. Development tends from simplicity toward complexity. The complexity of a message can be defined as the impossibility of programming it in a shortened form, that is, the lack of any algorithm simplifying the transmission and reception of the message. This definition was elaborated by Kolmogorov and Chaitin (see [48]). In other words, complexity means nonredundancy, that is, irreplaceability of the elements of a message. Complexity coincides with the value of information.

The ability of the developing biological system to select valuable information increases in the course of development. The loss of possibilities for adaptation connected with simplicity of structure and mutual replaceability of cells and tissues is compensated by the vital advantages of an autonomous, complicated system. The high degree of the system's independence of external influences arises as the result of selection of the valuable information. Selective ability is especially high in the case of higher animals, whose sensory organs are intended for just this goal. A frog reacts only to the moving insect; a bat or a dolphin using ultrasonic signals receives only reflected and not direct signals.

For many years the literature was replete with talk of the "antientropicity" of living systems. Attempts were made to describe them as possessing the properties of Maxwell's demon, that is, the ability to extract information from the surrounding medium and to lower its entropy without expending energy. These unsound ideas contradict the second law of thermodynamics. We always have to pay for the information obtained by an increase of entropy of some subsystem contained in a big isolated system. Thus, during the freezing of liquid (which means a decrease in entropy and an increase in the amount of information), the entropy of the refrigerator increases; the refrigerator is heated. In accordance with the second law of thermodynamics, this increase of entropy surpasses its decrease in the freezing liquid, and the net entropy increases.

As has been said, one bit of information is equivalent to a change in entropy of $k \ln 2$. This means to receive one bit of information, not less than $kT \ln 2$ of energy must be spent.

However, $kT \ln 2$ is the "payment" for one bit of any information, independent of its value—both for the valuable information and for the redundant, replaceable information. The selection of valuable information does not require any additional expenditure of energy. It is sufficient for such a construction of the channels in membranes that only molecules or ions of definite form and dimension can be transferred through them. Expenditures of energy connected with the formation of specialized channels or receptor sites at membranes have been made earlier, at the preceding stages of evolution.

From the point of view of information theory, the main features of the living system are the ability to create new information and to select valuable information at no additional expense.

We see that physics offers many opportunities for understanding life phenomena. There are no limits to the further development of biophysics. However, this development is at its beginning, and therefore it meets with many difficulties. In the next section we shall speak about one of these difficulties.

CHAPTER 13

About False Biophysics

We have presented a short review of the ideas and methods of contemporary biophysics, and we have covered its main trends.

However, it would be erroneous to think that the development of biophysics is without obstacles. True biophysics coexists with false biophysics, just as two sides coexist on a coin. Pseudoscience, a crooked mirror of true science, is a social phenomenon requiring attention.

Pseudoscience is easily recognized. An idea is suggested that lacks any serious theoretical and experimental argumentation, and is isolated from the mainstream of scientific thought. At the same time this idea contains high pretentions: as a rule the pseudoscientist is interested in general scientific problems and he promises to "revolutionize" both theory and application. The sources of pseudoscience are dilettantism and ignorance, neglect of rigorous theory and experiment, and ignorance of the preceding development of science. Sometimes the pseudoscientist is mentally ill. In Gogol's *Memoirs of a madman,* his hero Poprishtshin claims to be the king of Spain. Were this book written nowadays, he would probably claim to be a great scientist.

Biophysics has now become very important and hence fashionable. The appearance of pseudobiophysical works reflects the nonuniformity of development of physics and chemistry on one hand and of biology, agriculture, and medicine on the other. As we have seen, the creation of theoretical biology based on rigorous physics is at its beginning. In this situation, there is a trend to avoid difficulties in the interactions of physics and biology by using pseudoscientific speculation as if it can solve the complicated problems of biology, medicine, and agriculture.

When crops fail, pseudoscience steps in and promises to solve the problems of agriculture. This is the main cause of Lysenko's success.

During the last decades, several trends arose in pseudobiology and pseudobiophysics. We now list them.

Specific "antientropicity" of living systems. The concept of their especially high ordering was discussed in Chapter 9. This idea stems from misunderstanding of thermodynamics and information theory.

Special electronic properties—semiconductivity (and even superconductivity)—of biopolymers and of total biological systems. The fictitious notion of "biological plasma" is connected with these ideas.

The existence of fields that have been unknown to physics ("biological field").

The biological importance of specific kinds of weak radiation; "magnetobiology."

Specific properties of water in biological systems, in particular, the influence of "magnetized water" on the physiology of plants and animals.

This list is not exhaustive, but it represents typical trends of senseless investigations. Let us consider them in sequence.

The seeming contradiction between the development of ordering in phylogenesis and ontogenesis serves sometimes as a source of ideas about the nonvalidity of the laws of thermodynamics in their applications to living systems. Thus a book [49] (that appeared in both English and German translations!) claims that when life began, the applicability of thermodynamics to nature ceased; before that moment, thermodynamics was valid. These senseless ideas are refuted by the arguments presented in Chapter 9. We have seen that the thermodynamic treatment of biological phenomena is limited but nontrivial. Thermodynamics remains right, and of course the second law is correct both for the human organism and for the steam engine. Classical thermodynamics is right but not sufficient. For the understanding of life, irreversible thermodynamics and kinetics are necessary.

Erroneous understanding of nonequilibrium thermodynamics is the cause of serious mistakes of a different nature. There are attempts in the literature (see, for example, [50]) to describe the differentiation, morphogenesis, and growth of a multicellular organism with the help of the formalism of linear nonequilibrium thermodynamics. As we have seen (Chapter 9), linear thermodynamics is not applicable to the treatment of ordering processes. Zotin's work [50] introduces generalized "flows" of the changes of weight (growth), morphogenesis, and differentiation, and corresponding "generalized forces." The force causing differentiation happens to be time! Evidently such flows cannot be flows in the physical sense of the word, and the formal equations suggested by Zotin [50] lack any physical meaning. The only argument is that with the help of these equations, the author obtains the dependence of animal growth on time, which agrees with experiment if a series of parameters is chosen. This result has only empirical meaning, and does not support the initial hypothesis.

Sometimes we meet with assertions about specific flows of "biological information." This notion is introduced without scientific definition. The information becomes opposed to physicochemical processes and obtains totally fictitious character.

The ideas connected with the search of specific electronic properties of biopolymers arose many years ago in connection with publication of a book by the outstanding biochemist Szent-Györgyi [51]. At that time, the structures of proteins and nucleic acids had not been sufficiently studied. In his second book [52], the author himself characterizes his first book as a fantastic one. Nevertheless, works devoted to semiconductive and even superconductive properties of biopolymers continue to appear in the literature from time to time.

As we have seen, electronic conductivity along the polymeric chain is possible if the chain is formed by conjugated π-bonds. Such a chain possesses high rigidity and absorbs light in the long-wave (visual) region of the spectrum (see Chapter 2). However, there are no conjugated bonds in the chains of proteins and nucleic acids. The chains are colorless; they absorb light in the ultraviolet region of spectrum. Just because of the lack of conjugation, the biopolymers possess conformational flexibility and motility. There exists either semiconductivity or conformational behavior. All the data obtained in molecular biology and molecular biophysics testify in favor of conformational flexibility. The observed small electric conductivity of proteins is determined by ionic contamination and does not have any biological importance. Biopolymers are dielectrics.

From time to time, investigations of the so-called mytogenetic rays appear. The discovery of these rays was claimed by the outstanding soviet biologist Gurvitch in the twenties. It has never been corroborated by rigorous physical experiments, and there was almost no mention of it in the scientific literature of the following decades. Thus, in 1933 40 papers devoted to mytogenetic rays were published in the Soviet Union and 80 papers in other countries. In 1949–1956 there were only 20 papers published, and in the following 25 years this number did not increase. Sometimes it is said that the weak radiation of the vegetative and animal tissues in air due to the oxidation of lipids is mytogenetic radiation. This is not so; any organic substance can emit light in oxidative reactions. This radiation is of no interest to biology. It was claimed that mytogenetic rays are emitted because of the sharp hindrance of metabolism (for instance, due to cooling) or the mechanical disturbance of the spatial distribution of the system's cells. These nonexistant rays were called mytogenetic because they supposedly stimulate the division of cells!

The sad story of mytogenetic rays did not stop the appearance of publications about invisible rays of mysterious physical nature that transmit "biological information." We meet here with fantastic mysteries! There were Chizhevsky's "Z-rays" and Vassiliev's neutrino radiation of the brain, which determines extrasensory perception. Recently Kaznacheev's "death rays," emitted by dying cells, appeared. Kaznacheev claimed that the culture of cells perishing because of a viral infection emits some ultraviolet rays, which, when absorbed by a noninfected culture, cause the latter to perish in the same way. These rays could not be detected by physical methods. The described process contradicts elementary logic. Even if we assume that the death of cells causes radiation, it is impossible to understand why absorption of these rays by healthy cells must cause the healthy cells to perish. Exact experiments have refuted these claims.

"Invisible rays" are not new to physics. After Röntgen's great discovery, a series of invisible rays appeared. Seabrook's book about Robert Wood [53] describes how Wood unmasked the falsification connected with the so-called N-rays of Blondlot. The biological phenomena are extremely complicated. Therefore the unmasking of false experiments like that made by Wood is more difficult here.

There have also been reports on the reception of radio waves by organisms. The reports claim that the signalization of insects occurs with the help of radio waves. However, it was found long ago that this signalization is of molecular character; the corresponding substances (pheromones) have been isolated and their structures established. More than 100 years ago the great naturalist Fabre showed that the males of the *Saturnia* butterfly fly toward the chemical secretion of the female—toward the twig where the female had been sitting and even toward the chair where the twig had been before [54].

There are also kindred ideas about "biological radiocommunication" that explain telepathy, telekinesis, and other miracles [55].

The situation of electricity and magnetism in biology is rather bad despite such great events in its history as Galvani's experiments or the membrane theory of propagation of the nervous impulse. The cause is that electric and magnetic measurements in such complicated systems as cells and tissues can produce artifacts if knowledge and skill are not sufficient.

One book [56] states that at the body's surface, ions (either positive or negative) are collected. It is beneficial to a person's health to connect his body with the earth in order to discard excess ions. There are men who connect themselves at night to a central heating battery by a copper wire. All this has no scientific grounds. Suitable, reliable electric measurements have never been made. The importance of these hypothetical charges to medicine is more than doubtful.

We now cite some examples of nonscientific ideas relating to magnetism.

In one journal devoted to popular science, a paper was published describing "the effect of alternating field," whereby the magnetic field strongly influences cells and organisms, and "only the horizontal projection of the magnetic field possesses biological effectivity." This is explained by the occurrence in the cell of a totality of "elementary biomolecules"—their number is of the order of 10^9 per cell. Continuous motion of electrons along the rings occurs in these molecules. A "biomolecule" is similar to a gyroscope whose axis is oriented horizontally, that is, perpendicular to the force of gravity. Just because of this, the electrons of the "biomolecule" are influenced by the horizontal component of the magnetic field or, more precisely, the component of the changes in the field. "The information is brought into some biological object not by the external actions themselves but by their changes."

All this is rather far from being science. There are no "biomolecules" with a circular motion of electrons in nature. In the cell we meet with proteins, nucleic acids, carbohydrates, lipids, small molecules, and ions, and, most of all, with water, but not with "biomolecules." "Directioned motion of electrons" in a cell occurs only in the sense of directioned oxidative–reductive reactions in the membranes of mitochondria and chloroplasts. Should "biomolecules" really exist, they could not be oriented in the gravitational or magnetic field of the earth because this orientation would be disturbed by thermal motion.

What confirmations are there of this effect? In the same paper we read that medical observations show an increase in the incidence of heart attacks soon after the solar chromosphere flashes. How do these facts prove the existence of "biomolecules?" We read also about microbiological experiments concerning the reproduction of the phage lambda in *E. coli* under the action of a magnetic field. The description of these experiments given in the paper does not allow us to assess the degree of their reliability. Other confirmations are not cited.

Papers and books have discussed "magnetized water" and its biological role [57]. Let us first consider some properties of water, a substance crucial to biology. One of the false ideas concerning water is the supposition about the slow relaxation of water's structure: water can "memorize" what has been done with it. There are reports on the miraculous properties of melted ice and claims about the preservation of specific structure in this water; this is the reason why mountaineers who drink glacial water live long lives and children like to eat ice cream and suck icicles. These ideas are based on ignorance of facts well studied in physics showing that the relaxation times of water are of the order of nanoseconds. Experiments in which pure water was heated up to 300–400°C (under pressure) and subsequently cooled have been described [58], and it has been stated that the water "memorizes" the heating—the water becomes more acidic and the solubilities of some salts in it change. These properties can be preserved for a long time, but they disappear when water comes in contact with air. Evidently, the acidification of the heated and subsequently cooled water must be explained by some contamination by substances that are oxidizable or that interact with CO_2.

Let us return to magnetism. It is reasonable to discuss the possible influence of the magnetic field on cells and organisms. The magnetic field has almost no influence on diamagnetic substances—a category that covers most molecules with paired electrons, including all biopolymers. Diamagnetic susceptibility is very small, and the negative magnetization produced by it disappears with the velocity of light after the field is switched off. The paramagnetics—free radicals containing unpaired electrons, O_2 molecules, and some other molecules—become magnetized much more strongly, but in this case also the magnetization disappears with a rate determined by the thermal motion after the field is switched off. However, free radicals can appear in some biochemical reactions, and there exist chemical reactions whose intermediates possess the character of free radicals (triplet states). In this case, a magnetic field can influence the biochemical processes and, hence, the cells. In theory, this influence can appear even in weak fields. However, till now it has not been observed in biological phenomena.

Residual magnetization exists only in ferromagnetics, that is, substances such as metallic iron that possess a specific domain structure. Such substances have not been discovered in organisms. Only in the last few years have some species of the soil bacteria been found containing magnetite, and that is a very rare example.

Klassen claims that water, after being put even in a weak magnetic field, becomes "magnetized," and its properties change. Flowers grow better after being watered with it; it acts beneficially on the seeds of plants, sprouting them; it enhances "phagocytary activity of infusoria," possesses bactericidal action, etc. [57].

All these statements are based on very unreliable and unreproducible experiments. The only argument in favor of "magnetized water" is that according to some data, passing tap water through a magnetic field diminishes the amount of mineral deposits in boilers. Devices utilizing this property were patented long ago in Belgium and are used in some countries, including the Soviet Union.

Apparently, technology shows that the properties of water change under the influence of a magnetic field. The supporters of "magnetized" water write that this influence is determined by the "nonequilibrium" of the flowing water, by its ability to form "multimolecular structures," etc. This is pure fiction; it has no relation to science. Water is a diamagnetic substance that cannot "memorize" the action of the magnetic field. This argument shifts the apologists of "magnetization" to new positions. Well, say they, the field acts not upon water but upon the dissolved ions, which always exist in naturally occurring water. Physics shows that the magnetic field acts upon the moving ion with the Lorentz force equal to

$$F = KqHv \sin \alpha \tag{121}$$

where q is the ion's charge, H the strength of the field, v the velocity of ion, α the angle between the direction of the ion's motion and that of the field. K, as Klassen writes [57], is a coefficient.

However, the coefficient K is known. It is equal to $1/c$, where $c = 3.10^8$ m/s is the speed of light. In still water ions move at random, and their velocity averaged over all directions is equal to zero; therefore, the field H will deviate the ions with equal probability upward and downward, to the right or to the left. However, in flowing water there is a selected direction to the motion. Let the flow velocity of water be rather big: $v = 100$ km/h $\equiv 28$ m/s. We get $v/c \sim 10^{-7}$, a very small ratio. Thus the action of the magnetic field on dissolved ions is negligibly small.

How then can the removal of deposit (if such a removal really exists) be explained? We can readily see that such an effect can be connected only with the presence of the ferromagnetic particles in tap water. Any other explanation is a myth. Indeed, our statement has been found true. The mystery of the phenomenon has been cleared up through serious physical investigation [59].

Water forms deposits because at the walls of pipes, dissolved salts such as carbonates, sulfates, and silicates crystallize; if the water is a saturated solution of these salts (their solubilities are low). If the water contains a ferromagnetic admixture—some iron oxides and their hydrates—then their magnetization causes crystallization of the salts in the volume but not at the walls, and the diminishing of deposits. Evidently, the magnetized ferromagnetic particles stick together and form centers of crystallization. The problem was solved by a clear experiment; water containing salts but purified from the iron admixture to the degree that this admixture could not be detected by the methods of analytical chemistry, is not subject to any influence of the magnetic field. The amount of deposits cannot be lowered.

The problem is now solved, and it is classified in colloid chemistry. The sticking together of ferromagnetic particles produced by the magnetic field cannot influence anything except deposits. Therefore the statements about the invariably positive effect of the water "magnetization" which can enhance the production of concrete and bricks, improve flotation, catch dust, etc., are very dubious; and of course the sticking together of ferromagnetic particles has nothing to do with biology.

It is typical also that the supporters of the theory of "magnetization" of water either pass over in silence or mention casually the fundamental work [59]. This is understandable—the explanation of the ferromagnetic causes of the removal of deposits eliminates the possibility of water having "memory," nonequilibrium structure, etc. This explanation does not allow use of crop failures to promote pseudoscientific speculation.

"Magnetized" water is not the only fictitious substance existing in false biophysics. There are much more astonishing inventions. At least it is possible to ask reasonable questions about "magnetized" water and answer them experimentally. On the other hand, a substance like "biological plasm" lies totally outside the scope of science; nothing can be said about it. Yet this notion is sometimes used to explain some facts and many artifacts.

In a monograph devoted to "biological plasm" [60] we read the following:

1. Bioplasm [i.e., biological plasm] is the plasm (the fourth state of matter in physics) in conditions of the living organism.
2. Bioplasm is a thermodynamically nonequilibrium system that possesses a high degree of stability in the living organism.
3. Antientropicity is the inherent property of the bioplasm.
4. Bioplasm is the plasm at absolute zero. Of course the absolute zero is formed not because of the lowering of kinetic energy of the particles, but quite the reverse—because of the binding of the particles by complicated force lines of the fields that penetrate them.
5. The wave field is frozen into bioplasm . . . The united organismic hologram is formed. . . . Probably it is just the biological field.

Let us try to understand these statements. The plasm in physics is an ionized gas. Evidently such a gas cannot exist "in the conditions of the living organism." What, then, is bioplasm? What particles are contained in it? We do not find any answer to these questions.

The second quotation speaks about the thermodynamic nonequilibrium of the "bioplasm." As the definition of "bioplasm," its content, and its properties are totally mysterious, we can say nothing about it.

The third quotation introduces a new pseudophysical concept—antientropicity. What does it mean? In what units can it be measured? There are no answers to these questions either. Perhaps the fourth quotation will explain the meaning of "antientropicity." Here we meet with absolute zero—but not of temperature. What is the meaning of this absolute zero? What particles are "bound" by the complicated lines of force? What are the fields? The mystery deepens as in a Gothic novel.

Four new concepts appear in the fifth quotation: "frozen in" wave field, organismic hologram, biological field. The desire to put the questions vanishes—it is clear that we shall not get any answer to them. The quoted lines are written in a language totally alien to the language of science. The quoted text bears no relation to physics or biology.

What are the "experimental confirmations" of the bioplasm?

Bioplasm is confirmed by the existence of mytogenetic rays. We have already spoken about them.

Bioplasm is confirmed by the "Kirlian effect." When there is a coronal discharge, biological objects, such as the parts of the human body, radiate. The radiation of a person depends on his physical and mental state. It has been established that this dependence is connected with the moisture content of the skin. The radiation that accompanies a high-frequency discharge can be observed with any kind of object; it has no intrinsic biological character. Perhaps it can be used in empirical diagnostics of some diseases, but it has nothing to do with bioplasm.

Finally, the telepathy of plants is quoted as the proof of bioplasm! [60]. In a series of publications in some journals and newspapers, the "American scientist Baxter" is quoted as the observer of these extraordinary phenomena. It is stated that plants change their electric characteristics depending on the intentions and moods of men. The flower feels the mood of his host; it knows whether it will be watered or picked! More than that, the book [60] claims that plants react at a distance to the death of shrimps when they fall into boiling water!

Biological plasm is a senseless notion that lacks any definition and argumentation. Baxter is not a scientist but a police engineer, the inventor of the lie detector. The experiments concerning plant telepathy have no relationship with science; the corresponding reports can be used only as an April Fool's joke.

The discovery of the transmutation of elements in living organisms by "the American scientist Kervran" is a similar joke. The idea of transmutation of the elements in living nature was first introduced in a science fiction tale by Asimov about a hen that laid golden eggs.

The interconnection of various pseudoscientific notions in biophysics (and not only in biophysics) is very typical. The authors of corresponding writings always quote each other. The papers or books devoted to imaginary violations of the second law of thermodynamics are quoted in writings on bioplasm. In one small essay, we meet with the whole set of notions of false biophysics, including those of Kervran and Baxter [61].

We have described a part of the pseudobiophysical works written mainly in the Soviet Union; but pseudoscience is an international phenomenon, and similar ideas concerning biology and medicine can be met everywhere. It is sufficient to mention the so-called Phillipine medicine.

Of course, this chapter is not written for those who are constructing the curved mirror of biophysics; they are not receptive to criticism. This chapter is a warning. We conclude with the words of Lamarck: "Actually, because of the insistent requirements that hinder the acknowledgment of them as truths, many individual ideas, which are more or less likely but lack good foundation, become forgotten immediately after they appear. Of course, the same sometimes causes rejection of or inattention to outstanding views and serious opinions. However, it is better that the truth, once understood, be condemned to a long struggle without obtaining the deserved attention than that everything given rise to by the vivid imagination of man be believed" [62]. Without the high standards of theory and experiment, science cannot exist. The same is analyzed in detail in [63].

Finally, let us discuss a rather important question about the necessity of criticizing pseudoscience. Perhaps it has not been worthwhile to spend the time of the author and readers on this subject.

Let us discuss this problem in the traditional form of a conversation.

Conversations about Pseudoscience and Scientific Mistakes, Ethics, Aesthetics, and Other Important Matters

AUTHOR *is sitting and writing at his desk.* OPPONENT *enters. After friendly handshaking—they have known each other for a long time—the conversation begins.*

OPPONENT. What are you writing?
AUTHOR. It is a small popular book, *Physics and Biology.* See, I can show you the plan of the book.
OPPONENT. Oh, it is very interesting—but, wait! You call the last chapter of the book "About False Biophysics." It seems that you could not keep from attacking the so-called pseudoscience? I wonder why you do not become bored. Have you not made enough enemies already?
AUTHOR. I consider this chapter necessary. But I know that you are a liberal and do not agree with me.

OPPONENT. I can suggest no less than four weighty arguments against your struggle with false science.
AUTHOR. Let us hear them.
OPPONENT. First, the phenomena that you call false science do not exist by themselves but in connection with some defects in organization of scientific work and education. You do not touch them; you scratch only the peak of an iceberg—but without touching these general defects you cannot discuss false science.
AUTHOR. I cannot agree with you. False science is a universal phenomenon, and one of the most important causes of its success lies mainly in ourselves—in scientists who do not get over their own laziness and timidity, in scientists who do not possess a sense of humor. Following your logic, I must consider either all or nothing. You are wrong.
OPPONENT. Perhaps my second argument will be more convincing for you. Pseudoscience should be ignored because it cannot hinder genuine science.
AUTHOR. It is quite possible to hinder science.
OPPONENT. You have pronounced my third argument yourself. Announcing some ideas as pseudoscientific, it remains to strive for their prohibition. My friend, you must agree with me that this is dangerous. You do not know everything; what if you are mistaken?
AUTHOR. In contrast to scientists, pseudoscientists look for support outside the scope of science. I do not look for such support. I express my opinion only. I do not possess any might and I do not prohibit anything; but I can and I will refute their numerous articles, which appear mainly in nonscientific publications. I am writing not a directive but a warning.
OPPONENT. My fourth argument is the most important: you have to be more kind.
AUTHOR. Without kindness in the true sense of the word there is no human life, but kindness has nothing in common with laziness, timidity, and opportunism. Which is more kind: to express your opinion in a direct and sharp way or to send the work of a pseudoscientist to another specialist because "I am too busy?"
OPPONENT. I wonder whether it does not seem to you that the struggle with pseudoscience violates to some extent the principles of scientific ethics, freedom, and democracy, without which science cannot exist.
AUTHOR. I do not think so. Freedom and democracy mean that every author of a work has the right to attention and that his work

must be evaluated by specialists; but the same democracy means the right of specialists to criticize it and requires a serious and attentive attitude to such critics.

Concerning ethics, I must say that it is violated by the pseudoscientists themselves. They violate ethics using broad advertisement in the press and dishonest presentation of their own results and of the results obtained by others. It is typical that they begin to cry about ethics when they are caught.

OPPONENT. I am afraid that our discussion is rather futile without strict criteria for discriminating between pseudoscience and scientific mistakes, which are always possible.

AUTHOR. Scientific mistakes arise from the nonexactness of experiment or theoretical reasoning, but are never due to a deliberate attempt to reject the statements established by science. Such an attempt is typical of pseudoscience. Scientific mistakes can therefore be cleared up after some time, but pseudoscience is evidently without any control. Scientific mistakes are cleared up and corrected in the course of subsequent work, when the results obtained are discussed. A real scientist is sincerely interested in the removal of his mistakes and does not insist on them. In contrast you can never convince a pseudoscientist. This distinction has already been made by Kapitsa.

OPPONENT. Is the phlogiston theory mistake, error, or false science?

AUTHOR. This question is quite legitimate. Of course you cannot treat some theory or experiment independently of the time of its appearance. The phlogiston theory was, in its time, the first reasonable attempt to introduce a system into chemical knowledge. At that time the phlogiston theory was science—it gave valuable information. Later, however, it gradually became clear that the idea of phlogiston is erroneous. Should somebody try now to revive phlogiston theory, he would be a false scientist.

OPPONENT. What would you say about the "crazy" theory of Niels Bohr? There are cases when the truth becomes clear only after some time has elapsed.

AUTHOR. A theory that introduces new ideas can of course be considered crazy; but it is a scientific theory if it explains the experimental facts better than the previous concepts. So it was with Bohr himself: his orbital model of the atom was crazy in 1913 because it violated the laws of classical electrodynamics. However, Bohr's theory explained the atomic spectra quantitatively for the first time. The pseudoscientific theories and experiments explain nothing.

Science does not develop by discarding the truths that have been obtained previously but by including them in broader concepts. The development of science is irreversible, and it is impossible to destroy that what has been obtained by science and confirmed experimentally. Landau wrote: ". . . every logically closed theory, whose correctness has been proved experimentally with a definite degree of precision, never loses its significance, and every more exact new theory involves it as an approximate result, which is right in some particular cases." The general methodology of science, based on rigorous formulation of the problem, logical theoretical suggestions, and exact experiments, cannot be rejected.

OPPONENT. I do not dispute that; but it has happened several times that the great discoveries were rejected by contemporaries, even by good scientists. Let us remember that the academician Ostrogradsky did not understand the geometry of Lobachevsky, and that the excellent chemist Kolbe mocked at the works of Van't Hoff devoted to the arrangement of atoms in space.

AUTHOR. It is quite natural. Scientists are men and they can make mistakes. It is not important that Ostrogradsky did not understand Lobachevsky; it is important that Gauss did understand him. Real science cannot remain unrecognized for a long time, especially in our century; but a pseudoscientific work is acknowledged only by pseudoscientists, such as its author, or by ignoramuses.

An excited VISITOR *bursts into the room.*

VISITOR. I think you know me. You have treated my work in a nonrespectful and moreover in a rough way. I demand an explanation and an apology.

AUTHOR. I am sorry; I did not want to offend you, but I cannot add anything to my review of your paper. I really think that your work belongs to the pseudoscience and I have presented the necessary argumentation.

VISITOR. No, you must prove that I am wrong!

AUTHOR. I repeat that I have presented scientific arguments. By the way, I am not obliged to prove anything. There is no presumption of innocence in science.

VISITOR. What do you mean by that?

AUTHOR. The fundamental of justice is the presumption of innocence: the accused does not have to prove his innocence; the court has to prove his guilt. The situation in science is quite the opposite. There is a presumption of "guilt" in science. The author of a scientific work is "guilty" by definition. He must prove his rightness himself.

VISITOR. This reasoning has nothing to do with my cause. If you please, I am ready to repeat my experiments together with you.

AUTHOR. The false science in your work follows directly from the general physical concepts. Concerning joint experiments, I refuse. I cannot spend my time on experiments that I consider senseless.

VISITOR. Everybody can see that you have given yourself away! You have demonstrated your reactionary nature and your total neglect of scientific ethics! How can such a person be allowed to judge outstanding work!

AUTHOR. You are free to think and to say what you want; but I am judging only on the basis of my knowledge and experience.

VISITOR. You will be hearing from me! I shall complain! [*Exits in anger*]

OPPONENT. I wonder whether you get any pleasure from such visits?

AUTHOR. Honestly, not at all!

OPPONENT. Are you really right in refusing to make experiments together with him?

AUTHOR. Of course I am right. It is not easy to pinpoint the methodic error in the work of a pseudoscientist or a fraud. That takes a criminalist like Robert Wood or Kitaigorodsky. I am sure, for instance, that the illusions of Kio in the circus do not contradict the laws of physics, but I do not understand how he does them. Frankly, I have plenty of serious things to do instead of checking the experiments of our guest.

OPPONENT. Then you cannot criticize him.

AUTHOR. Really? If a man comes to you with a plan for a new perpetual motion machine, will you not immediately reject the project?

OPPONENT. I must show him where the mistake is.

AUTHOR. Not at all! Let him look for his mistake himself if he is an honest person.

OPPONENT. What can you say about the criterion of practice?

AUTHOR. We are speaking about it all the time. Evidently pseudoscience is rejected just on the basis of the criterion of practice in the broad sense of this word. As the physicist Migdal wrote, no checking is required in these cases; it has been done beforehand.

OPPONENT. I think that our guest would not have been so offended if you had spoken to him in a more respectful way. Truth is born in discussion.

AUTHOR. I have already disputed with him in the press. It is a useless job.

Concerning the truth, I must say that it is always good if it is not a commonplace truth—like your last statement about the birth of truth in discussion. Give me, if you please, a single example in the history of science when a dispute has produced the truth. Truth is born in serious work. Moreover, we cannot dispute truths rigorously established: the validity of the second law of thermodynamics, of the noninheritance of acquired characters, or of the multiplication table. Discussions and disputes are necessary in considerations of unsolved problems, the number of which is always greater than the number of solved problems.

OPPONENT. Still I must say quite openly that you put too much passion into your struggle with pseudoscience. Emotions are a bad leader in the solution of scientific problems.

AUTHOR. You are wrong. The aesthetic emotion is extraordinarily important in science, particularly in the struggle with pseudoscience. Truth is beautiful; pseudoscience is ridiculous and ugly. Therefore a sense of humor is essential in this struggle. What counts is not the passion, but the laughter.

You see, if my field were not biophysics, but let us say quantum mechanics, I would not write about false science. Ignorant attempts to reject quantum mechanics arise frequently, but they do not really need any attention.

The situation in biophysics is different. This science is at its beginning, and the muddy overflow of false science is here. Some people seriously study the "bioplasm" and the "extrasensory perception" of plants! Here is a real danger for science and culture.

OPPONENT. I see that I cannot persuade you. By the way, concerning plant telepathy—I recently read about it in a very popular journal. I think you would write about this paper.

AUTHOR. I shall see. Give me the reference.

OPPONENT. Surely I shall give it to you; but please do not mention my name. Greetings. And be careful! Carefully! [*Shakes hands; exits.* AUTHOR *shrugs his shoulders thoughtfully and returns to his manuscript.*]

References

1. N. Bohr, "Atomic Physics and Human Knowledge." Wiley, New York, 1958.
2. E. V. Shpolsky, "Atomic Physics." Nauka, Moscow, 1974.
3. N. Bohr, *Symp. Soc. Exp. Biol.* **14,** 1 (1960).
4. M. Volkenstein, "Cross-roads of Science." Nauka, Moscow, 1972.
5. F. Engels, "Dialektik der Natur." Gospolitizdat, Moscow, 1955.
6. N. K. Koltsov, "Organization of the Cell." Biomedgiz, Moscow, 1936.
7. E. S. Bauer, "Theoretical Biology." VIEM, Leningrad, 1935.
8. V. Volterra, "Leçons sur la Théorie Mathématique de la Lutte pour la Vie." Gauthier-Villars, Paris, 1931.
9. E. Schrödinger, "What is Life? The Physical Aspects of the Living Cell." Cambridge Univ. Press, London and New York, 1945.
10. M. Volkenstein, "Molecular Biophysics." Academic Press, New York, 1977.
11. B. Gray and I. Gonda, *J. Theor. Biol.* **69,** 167, 187 (1977).
12. M. Volkenstein, *J. Theor. Biol.* **89,** 45 (1981).
13. M. Volkenstein, "Enzyme Physics." Plenum, New York, 1969.
14. L. A. Blumenfeld, "Problems of Biological Physics." Springer-Verlag, Berlin and New York, 1981.
15. J. Watson, "The Double Helix." Atheneum, New York, 1968.
16. J. Watson, "Molecular Biology of the Gene." Benjamin, Menlo Park, California, 1976.
17. B. Katz, "Nerve, Muscle and Synapse." McGraw-Hill, New York, 1966.
18. A. Hodgkin, "The Conduction of the Nervous Impulse." Liverpool Univ. Press, Liverpool, 1964.
19. M. Volkenstein, "General Biophysics." Academic Press, New York (in press).
20. C. Villee and V. Dethier, "Biological Principles and Processes." Saunders, Philadelphia, Pennsylvania, 1975.
21. J. Bendall, "Muscles, Molecules and Movement." Heinemann, London, 1969.
22. I. Prigogine, "Introduction to Thermodynamics of Irreversible Processes." Thomas, Springfield, Illinois, 1955.
23. P. Glansdorff and I. Prigogine, "Thermodynamic Theory of Structure, Stability and Fluctuations." Wiley (Interscience), New York, 1971.

24. A. Zhabotinsky, "Concentrational Autooscillations." Nauka, Moscow, 1974.
25. G. Ivanitsky, V. Krinsky, and E. Selkov, "Mathematical Biophysics of the Cell." Nauka, Moscow, 1978.
26. J. Monod, "Zufall und Notwendigkeit." R. Piper & Co. Verlag, München/ Zürich, 1974.
27. Y. Romanovsky, N. Stepanova, and D. Chernavsky, "What is Mathematical Biophysics?" Prosveshtshenie, Moscow, 1971.
28. Y. Romanovsky, N. Stepanova, and D. Chernavsky, "Mathematical Modelling in Biophysics." Nauka, Moscow, 1975.
29. A. Andronov, A. Vitt, and S. Khaikin, "Theory of Vibrations." Fismatgiz, Moscow, 1959.
30. M. Volkenstein, "Molecules and Life. Introduction to Molecular Biophysics." Plenum, New York, 1970.
31. H. Haken, "Synergetics." Springer-Verlag, Berlin and New York, 1978.
32. E. Wigner, "Symmetries and Reflexions." Indiana Univ. Press, Bloomington, Indiana, 1967.
33. M. Eigen and R. Winkler, "Das Spiel." R. Piper & Co. Verlag, München and Zürich, 1976.
34. M. Eigen, *Naturwissenschaften* **58,** No. 10 (1971).
35. B. Dibrov, M. Livshits, and M. Volkenstein, *J. Theor. Biol.* **65,** 609 (1977); **69,** 23 (1977).
36. I. I. Shmalhausen, "Cybernetic Problems of Biology." Nauka, Novosibirsk, 1968.
37. A. Jaglom and I. Jaglom, "Probability and Information." Nauka, Moscow, 1973.
38. M. Volkenstein and D. Chernavsky, *J. Soc. Biol. Struc.* **1,** 95 (1978).
39. M. Bongard, "Problem of Recognition." Nauka, Moscow, 1967.
40. A. Kharkevich, "Selected Works," Vol. 3. Nauka, Moscow, 1975.
41. R. Stratanovich, "Theory of Information." Sovetskoje Radio, Moscow, 1975.
42. H. Quastler, "The Emergence of Biological Organization." Yale Univ. Press, New Haven, Connecticut, 1964.
43. A. Blok, "About the Destination of a Poet." 1921.
44. M. Volkenstein, *Nauka i Zhizn* No. 1 (1970).
45. M. Volkenstein, *J. Theor. Biol.* **80,** 455 (1979).
46. M. Kimura, *Sci. Am.* **241,** No. 5, 99 (1979).
47. M. Volkenstein, *J. Gen. Biol.* **42,** 680 (1981).
48. G. Chaitin, *Sci. Am.* **232,** No. 5, 47 (1975).
49. K. Trintsher, "Biology and Information." Consultants Bureau, New York, 1965.
50. A. Zotin, "Thermodynamical Approach to the Problems of Development, Growth and Growing Old." Nauka, Moscow, 1974.
51. A. Szent-Györgyi, "Bioenergetics." Academic Press, New York, 1957.
52. A. Szent-Györgyi, "Introduction to a Submolecular Biology." Academic Press, New York, 1960.
53. W. Seabrook, "Doctor Wood." Harcourt, New York, 1941.
54. J. Fabre, "La Vie des Insectes." 1911.
55. B. Kajinsky, "Biological Radio-Communication." Acad. Sci. Ukr. S.S.R., Kiev, 1962.
56. A. Mikulin, "Active Long Living." Fizikultura i Sport, Moscow, 1977.

57. V. I. Klassen, "Water and Magnet." Nauka, Moscow, 1973.
58. F. Letnikov, T. Kashtsheeva, and A. Mincis, "Activated Water." Nauka, Novosibirsk, 1976.
59. O. Martynova, B. Gusev, and E. Leontiev, *Usp. Fiz. Nauk* **98,** 195 (1969).
60. V. Injushin and P. Chekurov, "Biostimulation by the Laser Ray and Bioplasm," Kasakhstan, Alma-Ata, 1975.
61. G. Sergeev, "Biorythms and Biosphere." Znanie, Moscow, 1976.
62. J. Lamarck, "La Philosophie de Zoologie." 1809.
63. M. Volkenstein, *Nauka i Zhizn* No. 7 (1977).

Index

D

E

F

G

V

W

X

Z